Stop, Catastrophe Ahead!

By John Prutzman

"You can't go back and change the beginning, but you can start where you are and change the ending."

C. S. Lewis

John Prutzman

Please send comments and reviews to:
jmprutzman@gmail.com

Dedication

Dedicated to the Founding Fathers whose wisdom and insight into human nature bequeathed us a republic rather than a democracy. They created a self-regulating system of competing power structures based upon the rule of law. It works as long as the contending powers agree to abide by the rules. Let's hope that time has not passed.

Table of Contents

Acknowledgement

Thanks to all the people who have encouraged me to keep writing. And as always, special thanks to Edward Ingram and Terry Smith for believing in me at the very beginning of my journey and supporting my efforts. It's good to have encouraging friends.

Pt I: Gathering Clouds

Beginnings

The last decade has been a financial roller coaster ride for America. The bursting of the housing bubble led to a severe banking crisis that almost brought our financial system to collapse. We must go back to the Great Depression to see anything at all similar in American history. This crisis in America almost collapsed the world financial system because finances have become global in scope over the decades since World War II. Fortunately, we weathered the storm and returned to an era of anemic recovery for many years. The recovery finally gained real strength as taxes were cut and stifling regulations reduced. By 2018 unemployment reached historic lows, the economy gained strength, and the future seemed to promise good economic growth.

For those willing to see, this roller coaster ride has shown that both the world's financial system and America's financial system have a wide range of sensitivity to changes. Some changes don't seem to make much difference while others can and do precipitate a crisis. This implies our financial system is much more vulnerable to disruption than our normal, everyday experience suggests.

As humans we tend to think that if the good outweighs the bad (especially significantly outweighs the bad), then the situation is okay. But this is not the case for complex systems such as the economy. This may not be immediately obvious to you. Perhaps, it is more obvious when we look at a very familiar complex system, one we live with every day.

Just think of your body for a moment. It is definitely a complex system. You could live a productive and good life with only one eye or one arm. What happens when you have heart problems or brain cancer? You die prematurely. Complex systems tend to have small, even seemingly insignificant parts that must work properly or the whole system fails. This is why our economy is much more vulnerable than we assume as we go about our daily lives.

Economist like to tell us why the system acts as it does. They are even willing to make predictions for the future. But simple reflection on America's economic history ought to convince you that economists do a poor job of predicting a crisis and an even worse job of preventing them. But that does not mean nobody saw the problems coming. There are always a few, a distinct minority, that understand the logical outcome of trends. Generally, this minority is better able to account for human behavior.

So far, we can't reduce human behavior to equations, at least not yet. And economists do love to reduce the economy to equations. Equations are much easier to understand than the real economy. And making a prediction about the future is much easier using equations, even if they are incomplete or incorrect!

Hopefully you recognize the dilemma economists have when they study the economy. The basis of the economy is individuals going about their daily lives. At the very heart of the economy is the action of people! This means we must have at least some understanding of human beings if we ever hope to predict the future economy. But don't be confused. This is not the same thing as saying we need to predict the actions of every individual.

Perhaps an analogy might help our understanding. I assume you've taken a bath or shower recently. That water you used was made up of molecules of water (H_2O). You didn't know or care what each molecule was doing in order to enjoy the warm water. Now take water and put it in your freezer. I'm sure you expect it to turn into ice. If it doesn't, your freezer needs to be fixed! Again, you do not know or care what each water molecule is doing. You had complete confidence in saying the water would turn to ice. You made a prediction and it came true. You may even know that the water molecules slowed down enough to become orderly. But even if you didn't know this, the water still turned into ice.

In the same way, we can make some useful predictions based on human nature. We don't need to know what every individual is doing. We just need to discern the trend based on our understanding of human nature. Too often we like to blame unforeseen or negative circumstances on bad luck when it is really the result of human nature.

At its heart, this is not a profound idea. Blaming something on human nature means humans are just acting like humans. But that's the foundation we need to understand if we are going to understand where we are going as a nation.

In the following chapters we will consider some interesting aspects and results of human nature that are important for our discussion. These are the parts of human nature that we tend to be blind to in our own lives and the lives of others. They make it difficult for us to see the trends the small minority discerns. They make us vulnerable to the unseen and catastrophic.

Situational Awareness

On October 26, 1967, a Navy pilot flying an A-4E Skyhawk over North Vietnam was shot down by a missile. He spent the next six years as a prisoner of war being tortured from which he never fully recovered. After his release, the aviator admitted he had focused so much on the target he was assigned to bomb that he lost situational awareness. This happens when a pilot fails to keep track of what is happening around him. This is his important context. He needs to know what the other planes, both friendly and unfriendly, are doing. He also needs to know what the ground forces are doing to try to bring his plane down. In this case the pilot did not notice the oncoming missile and failed to take evasive action. It was a costly mistake for John McCain.

We can look at McCain's story and focus on his poor performance and the ensuing unlucky consequences. But if we do this, we will lose important context. Like McCain, we will lose situational awareness. We need the big picture view in order to fully understand McCain's actions. McCain was not the first fighter pilot in history. The story starts way back on December 17, 1903 with the flight of the first practical airplane outside Kitty Hawk, North Carolina. McCain was the recipient of almost 64 years of flying history. More to the point, much of the innovation and flying experience came from fighting wars: World War I, World War II, the Korean War, and Vietnam. The importance of situational awareness was learned the hard way during these wars and the military made sure to pass on this knowledge. McCain wasn't ignorant of the need for situational awareness. He made the mistake of ignoring it!

Unfortunately, as a society we also seem to have lost situational awareness. Like John McCain, we make the same mistake. We focus on present circumstances and forget what our past teaches us. Worse, we distort it, so we learn the wrong lessons. We lose the context we need for proper understanding.

This guarantees we will overlook or dismiss important information, which is the result of losing situational awareness.

Our relatively peaceful and prosperous life in America seduces us into believing we're on the right path as individuals and as a nation. We look to our abundance and prosperity and call ourselves blessed. We want to believe that our prosperity and peace are the ultimate signs that things are generally okay. But that does not mean we can't or won't make things better. We hope and expect our leaders to lead the way to a better future.

That's a problem. America faces a crisis because our leaders to a large degree have lost situational awareness. Unfortunately, those that are pushing for dramatic change, have forgotten or misinterpreted history. Worse they don't seem to consider the pitfalls inherent in human nature.

It is not a surprise that many Americans feel like our society has lost its way. There is a striking agreement on this point although solutions differ. Think of the problems that are in the news: immigration, gun control, diversity, gender, etc. These are worthy things to consider. But also consider that the real danger isn't from these problems. It's from the things not being considered! It was the lack of situational awareness that led John McCain to six years in prison. It's the lack of situational awareness today that can cause us as a free people to lose our freedom.

America stands at a critical point today. But that's too abstract a way of saying it. America is really the people in it. Better to say you and I and all our compatriots are at a critical point. And this requires us to change. Yet currently, we go through life oblivious to the danger before us and the change required. No, we ought not to be surprised when destruction overtakes us for it will when we lack situational awareness.

Loving Evil

Loving evil – "I don't love evil," you say. I'm sure you don't. I don't either. On the other hand, we know there is considerable difference in what people think is evil. One man's evil is another man's enlightened way forward. It almost seems pointless to talk about people loving evil since there is such variety.

Let me ask you, "Do you think it's possible to specifically define what things are evil and what things are good?" Given the variety of opinions, I doubt there can be any agreement on evil and good. But, it's not necessary to define specific cases of evil or good. Instead, we know people have a sense of right and wrong. Call it a conscience if you want. The specifics of the conscience seem to be strongly defined by culture. Different cultures geographically and in time have very different ideas of good and evil, but they all have a sense that there is right and wrong. And this leads to an interesting practical example that we can consider.

I used to live in the country outside Houston before the city expanded enough to have any effect on the area. On the way home there was a stop sign at an intersection with a major road. If I saw three cars pass the stop sign while I waited, it was a real traffic jam! Most times I didn't see any cars.

Come with me on a trip home late at night. I approach the stop sign and look and see a half mile in all directions. There's not a car headlight or taillight to be seen anywhere. It was just me, the empty road, and a stop sign. I'd like to tell you that I was always a law-abiding citizen and came to a complete stop at the stop sign. Alas, that wouldn't be true. Let's just say I rolled through the stop sign. I'll leave it to your imagination to decide what this means.

Was I obeying the traffic laws? No. Did I know it was wrong to continue without completely stopping? Of course! But I like to justify my actions, at least to myself, by saying I was being careful and safe. There was no actual need to have a stop sign late at night when there's only one car and empty roads. Was it still wrong? Sure! But the temptation!! I doubt there were many times when I came to a complete, legal stop. Rolling very slowly through a stop sign doesn't count as a stop even though it sure feels like it.

This points out the problem of loving evil. We all have done things we know we shouldn't have done. We do them anyway out of temptation, greed, anger, or any number of reasons. And there's always an element of self-interest. It was easier and less time consuming for me to roll through the stop sign rather than stop. My self-interest was more important to me than doing what was right. The ugly truth is that doing this often enough corrupted my conscience. It no longer bothered me when I rolled through that inconvenient stop sign. It was just a habit that required no thought. But it was still wrong!

Surely you can agree that for the most part we want to do what's right, but sometimes we really want to do what's wrong. And that's what I mean by loving evil: doing wrong when we know to do right. This seems to be part of our human nature.

If human nature is prone to do evil occasionally, then we should see this behavior in children as well as adults. It also means we don't have to teach children to love evil. I raised three children, and there were times when they knew what's right but chose not to do it. And this behavior was noticed within the first year of life. Can you remember your parents telling you not to touch something? Did you just walk away and think nothing more of it? Of course not! If anything, it created more desire to touch the object. The temptation was just too great. You reached out and touched the forbidden fruit, whatever the object was.

Maybe you don't remember any incidents like that. How about your parents telling you not to do something? Don't play in the mud, don't squeeze the cat, don't spend time with Billy. Make your own list and don't forget to add things you were told to do but you didn't bother. I'm sure you can think of something.

If you doubt what I am saying about loving evil try an experiment. Put a candy bar on the coffee table and tell a child not to eat the candy. Do you want to guess what will happen when you walk away? Most children haven't developed enough restraint to ignore the candy. It may start with just touching it, but it ends with a missing candy bar!

My point about loving evil is we don't have to teach children to do it. We must teach them to not love evil. And I find that same human nature still present in adults. At times our actions show we are all guilty of loving evil. Consider this: I didn't stop at the stop sign because I simply didn't want to stop!

Please do not be confused. We may love evil at times because it's in our nature to be tempted. But this does not mean we are inherently evil. It just means we sometimes choose the wrong way. And that is just our human nature at work.

We agreed at the beginning of the chapter that you don't love evil and I don't love evil. But this strikes me as a denial of an objective truth. Often this takes the form of outright rejection of the idea that mankind is inherently prone to evil. In this view, mankind is basically good and through discovery and education is bettering himself. There is some merit to this idea, but it can easily create confusion for us. It can justify rationalizing away our problem of loving evil by ignoring our desire to do what is wrong. We don't always do wrong out of ignorance. Sometimes we do wrong because we want to do wrong. More education doesn't necessarily change this.

In the incomplete view of progress, when a child does something bad, it is because he or she doesn't know any better and needs to be educated. When an adult does something wrong, it is because society is not yet perfect and has failed to educate and enlighten the evildoer. This is just a way of saying that the people around the evildoer are not sufficiently perfected and need to learn to do better. Doesn't this sound a lot like what happens in American society today? Society gets the blame for the evildoer's actions.

This incomplete view of progress implies that history is a long march toward perfection and that mankind can and will solve the problem of imperfect individuals doing evil. In this view enough enlightenment leads to better education, which naturally leads to less and less evil over time. Thus, mankind is on a march to perfection! This is admittedly a very hopeful view for individuals to have.

Someone believing in the "march to perfection" simply cannot admit that a truly enlightened person would ever choose to do evil. History does show we have made great strides in understanding and controlling the physical universe. An honest reading of history also shows that mankind has made very little, if any, real progress in the moral realm of forsaking evil. America has seen its recent share of political and religious leaders exposed for doing wrong when they knew to do right. They loved evil. Go back and think of the child who we are told just lacks education about what is good. The "march to perfection" fails to account for the fact that no one had to teach the child to do bad! The child naturally does bad sometimes. In that case it is the good that needs to be taught! This shows human nature has a natural tendency to love evil. No matter how enlightened or educated we are, if we are honest with ourselves, we must admit we willingly do wrong sometimes. And if we are especially honest, we must admit that we even have done some things wrong, knowing they are wrong, because we wanted to or simply chose to because it was the easiest action at the time.

One glaring problem we have in America today is our refusal to admit that all humans are prone to love evil. There is no group of especially enlightened people who have overcome this problem. This doesn't make everyone evil. It just means we routinely justify loving evil and ignore its perils. How easy it is to become self-righteous, especially if our goals are good! Do I really think I'm justified in running through stop signs? If I do it often enough, I will. Then the time will come when I run a stop sign when I shouldn't. And claiming the ends justified the means will bring small comfort to those involved in the accident! We'll have more to say about this later.

The problem of loving evil gets compounded because I don't want to hold myself accountable. I justify myself so I don't hold others accountable either. After all, my finger pointing at them has three fingers pointing back at me! If I think about it at all, I rationalize all the actions, theirs and mine. I think they are justified in their actions because I am justified in mine. But mostly I don't think too deeply about loving evil. Instead I just focus on the lovely thought that we are all making progress together to a better future, while I conveniently ignore a fundamental issue.

Does this sound familiar in America today? Do we really hold our leaders accountable for their actions? Do we even consider that our leaders are just as prone to love evil as we are? The truth is, it just seems easier to ignore this problem altogether. Let's just pretend all is well. Then we don't need to spend time and energy to correct the problem.

Much of the desire to change America is sincere but the proposed solutions neglect fundamental human nature. A recognition that we are all prone to love evil at times should make us realize we need a systemic solution for this. It is not enough to just pass laws to stop or penalize people who love evil. Someone must have the authority to pass these laws. Someone must also have the power to enforce these laws. And someone must have the authority to see that the law enforcement is done properly. If humans never choose the wrong way over the right way, then this authority can reside in one person or a small group. This has been tried in many places throughout history and the results have been less than perfect, and that's being very charitable. The truth is human nature guarantees such authorities move toward a system where the rulers prosper, and the rest suffer in some fashion.

Do you recognize that America has been moving towards concentrating power for many decades? Our federal government has become larger, more intrusive, and less accountable. Our business leaders have become super rich while the average worker has stagnated financially. This consolidation of power left unchecked cannot end well. It cannot end well because of basic human nature. Just think of history or think of Russia under communism or Venezuela under Maduro.

It may surprise you to know that Stalin did not amass a great fortune or live lavishly like his successors. But he still managed to kill between three and nine million of his countrymen. And he did it for what he considered a good cause.

He simply justified his actions as necessary for the greater good as he defined it. But there is no doubt that some of the greater good was simply his own personal greater good. He could not see that he was loving evil. But I hope you agree that the mass killing of millions of people is wrong. Stalin chose to do wrong but was blind to the truth.

The consolidation of power is always prone to bring corruption. Fast forward to Russia today. Putin had the choice to learn from the failure of communism. Instead he argued that the collapse of communism wasn't necessary. He thought the consolidation of power was good and necessary. Today Putin is a multi-billionaire and the average Russian is increasingly impoverished. Dissenters are routinely jailed or killed. The economy is run by oligarchs and decisions are routinely made for the benefit of the people in authority, not the mass of people in society. One word can sum this up: corruption.

History and contemporary times confirm that consolidating power into the hands of a few people never leads to good results precisely because humans are prone to love evil. Sometimes authority willingly chooses wrong over right. This is inevitable because of human nature. I know there is much debate in America today about what is right. This is a healthy exercise. What is not healthy and is pushing us towards catastrophe is our unwillingness to consider human nature.

I like to think we humans are making progress. We certainly have in the natural realm of physics, biology, medicine, etc. I fail to see progress in fundamentally changing human nature. Why else did we have Stalin, Hitler, and Pol Pot last century? Or why do we have Maduro in Venezuela or overbearing bureaucrats in America today? Human nature hasn't changed and none of the programs designed to help us choose right over wrong has changed this fundamental nature.

America's Founding Fathers were not perfect men and they never claimed to have created a perfect Constitution. They allowed for amendments in the future. What they did have was a realistic appraisal of human nature. Many Americans today focus on the shortcomings and sins of the Founding Fathers. The critics do this to argue that the Constitution is illegitimate and needs to be replaced. But notice that their arguments and solutions never address the fundamental problem that humans love evil at times.

Consolidating power to solve problems is itself problematic unless a systemic solution is included to prevent corruption. This is very difficult to do when we can only depend on humans, all of whom are prone to love evil. But this needs to be done to prevent corruption from spreading too far. Unfortunately, America has been failing to do this. But this only hastens the day when catastrophe strikes.

Pride

In the last chapter we saw that humans are prone to do wrong because there is a part of human nature that wants to do wrong. We called this loving evil. And loving evil always brings in corruption. But does this explain why a free people willingly let corruption flourish? Certainly, part of the reason must be that we excuse our own faults, so we overlook the faults of those in authority. We prefer not to be hypocrites. I'm okay, you're okay – even when we're not! This opens the door for corruption both in ourselves and in our society. And what form does that corruption take? Perhaps the most obvious form is pride.

Pride is an interesting word because it can mean either a positive thing or a negative thing. We understand that a workman should take pride in his work meaning the work should be as excellent as the worker can produce. By contrast, we have all met pride-filled people that are overbearing and unpleasant to be around. This kind of pride exalts self and is inherently self-centered and selfish. The former kind, proper pride, focuses outside of self on the work being done and produces a blessing (whether always recognized or not). The latter kind, selfish pride, destroys relationships and ruins trust. That's corruption at work.

In this chapter we are not concerned about proper pride, good pride because it is not a problem that would cause America to stumble. No, we are focused on the self-centered pride that goes before destruction. Unless we awake from our slumber and deal with our unwarranted self-centered pride, destruction will come to America. We need to recognize that a tendency to self-centered pride is inherent in our fallen nature and is something that is not a trivial issue.

Pride brings a desire to exalt oneself. It ultimately leads to a sense of entitlement, which we will discuss in a later chapter. Maybe you are thinking that you do not suffer from self-centered pride. Let me ask you, do you like to share with other people your financial difficulties, marital problems, struggles at work, problems with your children, etc.? These are things you might discuss with a few close friends or with someone giving counsel but not with everyone you know. You want to keep up proper appearances! Why is this? Because we don't want people to think poorly of us! We don't want them to think we have failed or fallen short of the mark. We would much more prefer them to think we are successful. We know they will treat us more positively if they think of us positively. But this just means we want to exalt ourselves in their sight! That is pride.

Notice that pride causes us to cover up truth and avoid dealing with it. As long as our problems remain hidden, we can put up a good front and live a respectable life. No one else needs to know about our struggles. At its worst, pride can blind even ourselves to the truth. We fail to even acknowledge there is a struggle or simply say the problems are all other people's problems.

Unfortunately, pride doesn't stop with our personal lives. We carry our self-centered pride over into our work. And it doesn't stop even there. It gets injected into our politics. We start electing politicians who will help us look good outwardly. We conveniently overlook their faults even when they take advantage of our human nature. This can never end well. Consider that we don't like politicians who tell us the truth and make us face reality!

For some time now, at the national level, we have elected politicians from both parties who will promise us more benefits and relieve us of more of our personal responsibility. We justify it to ourselves by thinking we are just being compassionate to the less fortunate. In our pride, we are well pleased with ourselves. We congratulate ourselves for building such a caring and compassionate nation. But we have ignored the truth that our politicians are tempted to love evil just as we are. And our misplaced pride has let corruption flourish.

Our pride tells us that corruption is not a big issue for America. Unfortunately, reality has a way of catching up with us. Our self-centered pride left unchecked leads to corruption that ultimately brings us dishonor and diminishes us. This is true in our personal lives but is also true in our national life as well. As we have insisted on acting with pride, corruption has increased in the corporate and political areas. Do you doubt this? Do you remember the Animas River toxic spill caused by the EPA? Some 3,000,000 gallons of water laced with mercury, lead, and other toxic heavy metals flowed down the Animas River into New Mexico polluting the drinking and irrigation water for the area. It happened in August 2015 when an EPA worker caused a leak in an abandoned mine. Did the EPA hold anyone responsible? No! Did the justice department prosecute anyone as they should have? No! In contrast, supervisors off duty and at home have been sent to jail for toxic spills of less than 5,000 gallons caused by others! There is no doubt that blind justice has been corrupted. The government has refused to hold itself accountable, but it will hold you accountable – even if it's not your fault!

Make no mistake. The Animas River toxic spill was a major disaster. But it wasn't the biggest disaster of that whole episode. The biggest disaster was the refusal of the American people to rise up and demand accountability. Our tolerance for corruption has increased that much. And that's the problem with corruption. We become insensitive to it the longer we tolerate it. Remember my stop sign story? After rolling through the stop sign, it becomes easier the next time. After a few times, my conscience didn't bother me as much. It's not too much of a leap to see we have not even begun to contemplate how low America can go as we let corruption flourish because of our pride!

I hope you see that self-centered pride is never a good thing and can only bring dishonor and destruction. So far, Americans have not acted like we believe this. In our pride, we act like we are somehow exempt from corruption. It has blinded us to the truth. Our pride has caused us to exalt ourselves above human nature as though we have transcended it. Left unchecked, there comes a day when our self-centered works and our myriad accomplishments will be seen for what they are: attempts to exalt ourselves above human nature. In that day we will be humbled, and our human nature will be shown for what it really is. That's the real story behind the Animas River spill. And that will be the story behind the catastrophe awaiting America.

You may be having a hard time accepting this. But consider that we have seen precursors to the coming disaster. We had the dot-com bubble crash in 2000. This was followed by the financial crisis of 2009 brought on by the crash of the housing market bubble. These are simply manifestations of our human nature at work. But we have failed to learn this truth and instead have looked for superficial causes and superficial solutions.

Since pride has a way of blinding us to the truth, it is very difficult for us to avoid the coming day of reckoning. But in truth, we cannot afford to build a system that neglects human nature. Yet that is exactly what we have been doing in America. We have allowed our leaders, our elite, to create a system that is becoming less and less accountable. The natural result is more and more corruption. But this is not the only problem. Our self-centered pride inevitably leads us into presumption and entitlement, which are topics of future chapters.

Pride is leading us down the path to destruction. This means every day we have a choice to make. We can choose to humble ourselves and create a nation that recognizes and accounts for human nature. Or we can continue to let pride blind us, ignore human nature, and let the circumstances of life humble us. It's our choice.

Let's choose wisely!

Presumption

In the previous chapter we asked why would a free people willingly let corruption flourish? As we noted, our self-centered pride blinds us to the truth. One of the ways it blinds us is through presumption. What do we mean by presumption? It is assuming or taking for granted something in our reasoning. We assume something is true without facts or proof. This is one of the explanations for why we have a difficult time believing any prediction of impending doom. We presume our life will be relatively stable, much as it has always been.

Experience has taught me that sometimes presumptions are not warranted. Have you ever tried to give helpful advice to someone only to have it totally rejected? Why do you think that was? Consider what we mean when we say, "helpful advice." What makes it seem helpful to us is that we believe it will help the person reach a goal we think is desirable. And that means we have presumed to know the proper outcome. The person may not agree with us. They may have a different goal in mind. That's one reason the person may reject our advice.

Let's explore this further. Think about addictions for a moment. To make it easier, consider a very common, acceptable addiction: smoking. There are plenty of good reasons to give up smoking. The benefits for the individual are overwhelmingly positive. Encouraging a smoker to quit seems desirable. But have you ever tried encouraging a smoker to give up smoking only to have the person reject this advice and act offended? The person may want to quit smoking, but the addiction craving is too much to withstand. Our advice failed to account for the full effects of addiction and the motivation caused by the craving it produces. We presumed we know best, but our presumption has made us short-sighted.

Too often without meaning to, we fall into the trap of presumption. In our previous example of smoking, I hope you see that presumption led us to try to control the agenda. Before we started offering our advice, we already had chosen the proper outcome. Moreover, we have even chosen the proper course of action. Our "helpful advice" points out the agenda we want the smoker to follow. The only reason smokers don't get offended more often by our presumption is that they feel guilty about smoking – they know it's bad for many reasons. In such a case, our presumption has blinded us to the motivation of guilt. I doubt we gave our "helpful advice" in order to make the person feel guilty. But provoking a person's feeling of guilt is not a very good way to offer helpful advice!

Lest we misunderstand, we need to make clear that living life requires us to presume things in order to be successful. It's not always wrong to presume. Start with the obvious. I presume the sun will come up tomorrow just as it did this morning. (It will.) I presume that the salesperson in the store speaks English. (It's true in most stores.) I presume people drive their cars obeying the rules of the road. (Hopefully!) But clearly in the last case, this is not always true, so I drive defensively.

It should be obvious that there are some things we can presume and others not so much. For instance, I presume I need to dress every day to go out in public. But there are other things which we presume that can easily cause us problems. Think about American prosperity. Since World War II, America has prospered. That means most people alive today did not go through the Great Depression or the War. This has caused many people to presume that America will continue to prosper. (Another depression? What's that?) We presume America will have prosperity and peace because that's what we've had for many years. Unfortunately, the recent past is not always a good predicter of the future. Presuming continued prosperity inevitably leads us to feel entitled to prosperity. We'll discuss the problems entitlement causes us in a later chapter.

At this point, we need to understand that presumption can be both good and bad. It is good when it helps us to make proper decisions. It's bad when it causes us to make wrong decisions. It's also bad when it leads us into disputes about reality. It may not be obvious to you, but presumption, especially misplaced presumption, leads to increasing conflict.

Often this happens because different groups have different presumptions on how people are expected to act. Within one group, these presumptions work well. But different groups can have different expectations, and that leads to conflict. A lot of the conflict we see in America today is because there is a mismatch in presumptions.

The only way a society can be cohesive is with a set of presumptions that all (or at least most) of the groups have in common. But this is precisely what is being sacrificed in America today. Many of the presumptions from the past are being challenged. Think about these recent and current conflicts:

1. The definition of marriage
2. The definition of gender/sex
3. The meaning of equality
4. The meaning of patriotism

I'm sure you can think of others. Unfortunately, a lack of common presumptions only gives rise to chaos. And chaos destroys trust, which we will discuss in detail in a later chapter. Without trust we can't have healthy social interactions.

Life requires that we be realistic. We can't live in chaos, so we need presumption. But remember how we started this chapter. We can't possibly know all the facts. And we certainly can't know in-depth the motivations of other people. Sometimes they just seem to do inexplicable things. And we don't always know the right way, whatever the "right way" really means. All this calls for humility in our dealings with other people. And humility is in short supply today.

Since World War II, America has become prosperous in the natural realm and impoverished in its presumptions. This is leading our society into more and more chaos. And our presumption that America will continue to do well is just that. It is a presumption that history suggests is unwarranted. Do we really want to live life like prosperity and good fortune will always continue forever? Such a presumption cannot serve us well. It blinds us to the truth. It certainly can't save us from what is to come because it is part of the problem. We simply don't see the catastrophe that is building. Catastrophe can happen – to America and presumption can't stop it!

Balance

In the last chapter we saw that today America suffers from unrealistic presumptions. Worse, it suffers from fundamental disagreement about basic presumptions. This is especially bad because any stable society requires a basic set of presumptions that most people in the society believe in and act on. Unfortunately, the breakdown we see today in presumptions only leads to conflict and increased chaos. And no nation can survive living in chaos.

I hope you see that between the opposite poles of chaos and our self-centered presumptions, there must be a third way. Life is a walk of balance between chaos and unwarranted presumption. Unfortunately, as humans we tend to lose our balance and fall into one or the other. It is balance that is required for us to be successful. This calls for some explanation. Let's look at this in more detail.

We presume life today will be like life yesterday and the day before that. I think we can agree this is a sensible way to go about life. I'm not planning for a tsunami or earthquake to happen in Houston today (or even tomorrow!). And I'm certainly not planning for the sky to fall at any time in the future. It is appropriate to assume life will carry on as before. This is an inherently balanced view of life and makes a lot of sense. Such a balanced viewpoint gives us the best chance at living a fulfilling life.

But I hope you can see that there is a vulnerability in assuming life will carry on as before. Houston may not have tsunamis or earthquakes, but it does have hurricanes. Just because it happens only occasionally doesn't mean I should ignore the possibility. I can at least have contingency plans, but so many people in Houston don't. Why? Because it's not part of their everyday life! Hurricanes always give us some warning of their approach thanks to our weather service. Truthfully, I don't need to plan for a hurricane today, tomorrow, or even this week.

Yes, we need to have a balanced view of life but it's not always clear what needs to be included in determining that balance.

Let's start by examining the balance between the two extremes we have been discussing: good times versus catastrophe. One extreme is to assume the good times of today will always continue. But this is not a balanced view of life. It's unbalanced because it assumes low probability (hurricanes) or unique events (catastrophe) won't happen. I wasn't alive for the stock market crash of 1929 and the Great Depression with 25% unemployment, but both happened. The truth is American can have a catastrophe. Our problem as humans is that it's easy to presume catastrophe won't happen because it hasn't happened before in our lifetime. But bad things can and do happen!

What is the opposite of presuming good times will always continue? The other extreme is to presume a catastrophe must happen. This is what doomsday cults believe. I don't subscribe to this opinion and I hope you don't either. I'm not preaching a doomsday cult. I simply wish to point out trends and problems that left unchecked will lead to catastrophe. In this case, the proper balance we need is to presume a catastrophe can happen, but that it's in our power to change that outcome. This can be a difficult balance to achieve.

Proper balance can be hard to achieve because presumption has a way of clouding our judgement. For this reason, we need to examine our presumptions. This is true for us as individuals and as a nation. There are many practical examples of the problem presumption creates. For example, the majority of people presume the government wants to help us. This is certainly true some of the time and in some ways. But it cannot be true all the time. Why? Because humans have an innate desire to control situations.

Think about the worst job a human can have. It is one that makes the person accountable for results but gives him no control over the outcome. This creates unrelenting and unbearable stress. It can and does wreck relationships and physical health. Humans naturally try to control the situation to prevent this from happening.

Think about the human nature of people doing government jobs. Theoretically they are there to serve you and me. But their human nature propels them to assume control rather than grant you control. Have you ever experienced frustration dealing with government bureaucracy? If you did, then you didn't have much, if any, control over the outcome! I bet the situation was stressful! And the government worker was much less stressed because he or she knew they controlled the situation.

Our presumption about the goodness of government fails to account for things that are likely to happen. It is inherently an unbalanced view. It does not account for basic human nature. Presuming government is always benevolent is not based on likely events, but on very unlikely ones. Such a presumption blinds us to the truth and causes us to make suboptimal or wrong decisions.

I previously mention the dot-com crash and the housing crash. I can safely predict a similar financial crash of some sort will happen again. Why? Because this is how human nature works. I may not know what the immediate cause of the crash will be. I may not know the timing. But I know it will happen. And I can't assume the government will make sure it doesn't become a real catastrophe. That's balance!

Increasingly Americans presume human nature has changed for the better. At least that's what their actions show. The truth is, we cannot presume our government is a benevolent, disinterested third party that will automatically do what's best for us as individuals or for society in general. Nor can we presume that we can safely weather any financial crises just because we came through the dot-com and later financial crisis. You and I didn't live through the Great Depression with 25% unemployment, but we shouldn't presume it won't happen to us. Indeed, we shouldn't presume that something worse won't happen. That's proper balance.

If we learn anything from this chapter, let's learn that presumptions are based on past experiences and likely events. They tell us little or nothing about infrequent or unusual events that can and do happen. We should also learn that our presumptions often don't account for basic human nature – human nature as it actually exists and not as we presume it to be or want it to be. We need to understand that faulty presumptions lead to bad outcomes eventually. It can't be otherwise.

America is headed for disaster because we haven't learned or have chosen to forget that balance is required between unwarranted, self-centered presumption and chaos. Either is detrimental. We need proper balance between these extremes. This requires us to examine our presumptions and make them conform to reality. We can't have a healthy society otherwise.

Entitlement

In a previous chapter, we saw that each one of us has a nature that is prone to willingly choose the wrong way on occasion (or even frequently). And we're very good at justifying it to ourselves. This is especially true when the results are good or positive. But our choices do have consequences and if we are not careful, we will find ourselves letting the end justify the means. Unfortunately, this leads almost inevitably to the corruption of our soul.

A natural consequence of corruption within our soul is the corruption of our society. Corruption in ourselves and in society is a lot like a disease. I can survive a cold and prosper. I may survive cancer or maybe not. I surely don't want to see if I can! How much corruption can our society withstand? It's not a good idea to test the limit to find out!

Corruption always brings disintegration into our lives so that we cannot function properly as individuals. Corruption in a society causes it to function poorly. In extreme cases, society can completely fail. Just look at what is happening in Venezuela today (2019) or the Soviet Union in the twentieth century. We have only to look around the world to see examples of societies with varying amounts of corruption.

I invite you to look around America today, and ask yourself if it appears to function properly. Do the people in authority seem less helpful, more self-serving, and outright corrupt these days? We've always had some corruption in our society given human nature. But today, there are more areas of authority that can be corrupted. Just look at the size of the federal government. Or consider the size of college and university bureaucracies. The latter have experienced a dramatic increase in administrators but not teachers. The administrators don't come cheap and neither does the cost of college.

The corruption we see has grown because our pride coupled with presumption has caused us to fall into a trap. It is the trap of thinking we are entitled to things. Naturally, the people in authority have used this sense of entitlement to gain more control over us. How? When I think I am entitled to something, I naturally think not only that I should have it, but that it rightfully belongs to me right now. Unfortunately, our human nature breeds this sense of entitlement, which blinds us to the truth.

Let's look at one example in America of entitlement that has opened us up as a people to disintegration and destruction. If you will, consider social security. On the surface this sounds like a beneficial thing for Americans. In exchange for regular contributions from our wages, the government agrees to pay us upon retirement and for the rest of our life, a monthly amount based on our contributions. Surely, we must be entitled to this benefit if we make the contributions as required.

Before social security was set up, tests were conducted that showed needy individuals would be grateful for benefits from the government only for a few months. After that they would feel entitled to the benefits and be resentful when they didn't get it. Politicians counted on this fact to create a system that would be difficult to change or end. They purposely designed the system to apply to a large segment of society, not just the needy. This guaranteed a large group of "entitled" people.

Do you see how clever this is? If you pay into the system, you feel entitled to receive something when you retire. You will resist any changes that mean you receive less money. That's why social security reform became known as the third rail of politics. Any attempt to make changes to social security meant political suicide.

On its face, social security seems like a compassionate and caring program. Apparently, it never occurs to most people that this seemingly good program might be a form of corruption that continues just because people do feel entitled. But what exactly are people claiming title to that is corrupt? They are not claiming title to their deposits with interest or appreciation.

They are claiming title to the money being paid in by current workers!

I'm guessing that a great number of readers don't see any corruption in this practice. Maybe we need to look at another example to see more clearly where our sense of entitlement has led us. Do you remember Bernie Madoff? He created an investment fund that operated the same way social security operates. What did he do and where did it lead?

Bernie Madoff created an investment company that year after year returned 10% or greater profits regardless of what the economy or markets were doing. How was this possible? Like social security, he used the current investor's money to pay the earlier investors profits. This worked as long as the amount of investment money coming in continued to increase, which is an impossibility. Madoff created a classic Ponzi scheme. Of course, he lived a lavish lifestyle right up until there wasn't enough investment money coming in to pay out the promised profits to earlier investors. His investment fund collapsed, and investors lost an estimated $48,000,000,000 ($48 billion). It was by far the largest Ponzi scheme in America. I hope you see that Madoff had created a giant fraud. It was corrupt at its very core.

Do you remember I said Madoff had a system similar to social security? We can see the corruption in Madoff's actions, but we fail to see the same corruption when it comes to social security. Our sense of entitlement to social security money blinds us to the corruption involved. Madoff cost investors $48 billion. Social security has unfunded liabilities of $15.8 trillion! This is almost 300 times as large. And just like Madoff, the government has siphoned off social security money year after year to spend on profligate programs. Worse, the government has taken all the excess funds while Madoff took only some of it. Madoff went to prison when his Ponzi scheme collapsed. What will happen when the social security Ponzi scheme collapses?

Our pride and sense of entitlement have led us to believe we are entitled to riches and blessings. These blinded investors to the corrupt Ponzi system of Bernie Madoff and it blinds us to the corrupt Ponzi scheme of social security. Consider that if an insurance company or other financial institution went to market with social security as a product, they would face criminal and civil penalties. Yet, we not only allow the government to exempt itself from the laws applied to normal businesses, we applaud their effort on our behalf. We convince ourselves social security is a compassionate system and seem determined to continue that right up to the time it collapses.

Social security is just one example of our sense of entitlement in action. What other things do we Americans feel entitled to? In a general way, we feel entitled to prosper. The result of that entitlement is a desire to make the government or other third party pay when bad things happen. An example of this is the federally subsidized flood insurance program. We buy flood insurance the government subsidizes because as individuals and families, we couldn't afford the actual cost of such insurance. We feel entitled to government help even though floods and hurricanes are part of nature. We feel entitled to build wherever we want and then expect others to help pay for the inevitable disaster when it comes.

Our sense of entitlement has led to a very unbalanced view of life. We sue doctors when a baby is born that is not perfectly healthy. We sue drug companies when the results of taking medicine are less than perfection. We feel entitled to good health and a perfect outcome from our physical afflictions until we are old. Good health is a desirable goal, but it isn't something we are entitled to. Yet, we are prone to look to the doctor, the insurance company, or the government to pay for ill health simply because we feel entitled to make them pay. The sad truth is there is not enough money in the country to pay for all the possible medical treatment that could be done.

Let me give you a concrete example of this truth. In 2011 my late wife was suffering from systemic scleroderma. It caused her stomach and intestines to stop functioning. She was literally starving to death. Every night I made sure she was fed intravenously. The cost for this nutrition was $3,000 per week for the last five months of her life. I certainly didn't have $65,000 I could put towards her treatment. And this didn't include the oxygen, doctor charges, medicine, or hospital charges. I was grateful to pay $1,200/month for catastrophic medical insurance and have the Minnesota government pay the actual medical charges.

Yes, I was grateful for the medical insurance, but I realize I felt entitled to this insurance because it was made available. As a people, we have demanded government provide us relief from our medical misfortunes. We like to think we are compassionate and caring towards others. This may be true but consider that something like 80% of all Medicare costs are consumed by people in the last six months of their life.

The sad truth is that all that expensive care didn't stop my late wife from dying at age 62. I'm glad for the extra few months we had together. Yet, I can't help but think our society can't afford to be so generous to everyone. I paid only a small portion of the actual care for my wife. Other people paid for it through their taxes. And I can guarantee that these people assumed government benefits would be available for them in the future. Do you see how this too is a well-disguised Ponzi scheme? The sad truth is there just won't be enough money available as our population ages. Our sense of entitlement will more and more come into conflict with our reality. And that's the heart of the problem with entitlement. It blinds us to reality!

American Idolatry

Americans pride and sense of entitlement have led us to make some things in our lives into idols. What do I mean by an idol? I mean something that takes a central place in our lives and is given great importance. They are things that influence our thinking and guide our actions

Money

Did you immediately think of money as an idol? That is certainly the first thought I had. Perhaps this thought comes because we have been such a prosperous nation for so many years compared to much of the world. We pride ourselves on our free enterprise system and our rags to riches stories. It is very appealing, and it is easy to see how this could lead to money dominating our lives.

It is no surprise that commerce, making money, proves to be such a big snare. Commerce has made us relatively rich. It has allowed us to have leisure time. It has given us better health, more choices, and less stress regarding survival. And at the heart of commerce is money.

Think back on Bernie Madoff. He may have seemed like a benevolent older man helping others with their investments, but his love of money became an idol and filled him with violence. He stole peoples' money leaving some of them completely destitute. Many worthwhile charities were left in financial shambles when promised money could not be given – Madoff had taken it. Some of his innocent employees were stigmatized and were unable to find work in their profession after the collapse. Finally, one of his sons who reported him to the authorities was so enmeshed in the fallout that he despaired and finally committed suicide. Violence indeed, thanks to Bernie Madoff. He was no better than the robber who pulls a gun on you and demands all your money. Or maybe he was like the blackmailer who bleeds you dry over time. Either way, you end up poorer.

Unfortunately, America has become infected with an emphasis on money. There is nothing inherently wrong in wanting to prosper. But it shouldn't become an idol that leads us to take advantage of people and outright harm them. Do you remember the Bill and Hilary Clinton Whitewater investment scandal from Arkansas? One tragedy that came out of that has stayed with me all these years. A retired couple bought a house from the development company and paid their mortgage faithfully until the last year of their thirty-year mortgage when they missed one payment. The couple didn't realize the mortgage papers said if any payments were missed, all the payments would be considered rent. Instead of owning their own home, they lost all the equity. Does that sound fair to you?

I hope you realize that a mortgage clause that can turn your equity into rent proves that money is more important than people. Only a person or corporation that has made money an idol would think it was acceptable to harm people in such an underhanded way. Was it legal? Sure, but it demonstrates my point about money becoming an idol to too many Americans.

Money idolatry causes us to do things that destroy trust. Trust is something we will have more to say about later. Here I simply want to point out that destroying trust has a negative financial effect. America as a nation can withstand a Bernie Madoff if justice is ultimately done, which it was. What happens in a country where justice isn't enforced? Think of Russia today run by the oligarchs and Putin. The standard of living is dropping, and the average Russian is becoming impoverished. It is safe to say that money is a big idol for those leading Russia.

America is not unique in letting money become an idol. Human nature has not changed in thousands of years of history. During times of prosperity mankind always seems prone to make money an idol. It's interesting to read the history of Israel given in the Old Testament. As the nation prospered, they always turned away from God, which then brought on destruction. You don't have to believe in God to see that prosperity caused the Israelites to abandon the very traits that led to a successful society.

This should be a warning to America. Our success as a country was not built on money as an idol. Idolizing money causes us to abandon the very traits that led to our success. Our country was founded on hard work and thrift because there wasn't a lot of wealth to pursue. It's hard to idolize money when there isn't much of it available!

Remember we said idols take a central place in our lives and are given great importance. They influence our thinking and guide our actions. Think about Whitewater investment and Bernie Madoff again. These were not built on hard work and thrift. Instead they were built on a desire to make lots of money and a willingness to harm people to get it. And that's what a money idol does to us over time.

Youth

America has chosen to make youth and youthfulness a cornerstone of our culture. Our emphasis is on staying young, which is impossible, so we settle for looking as young as possible. Think of all the commercials you have heard or seen to get rid of wrinkles or spots. How many commercials to help you lose weight or stay fit? There are commercials for bright smiles, ditching glasses, and hip, cool cars. And every one of them aims at making you look or feel young and successful. Whatever happened to wisdom, wisdom gained through experience and many years of living and learning?

Wisdom is more than mere knowledge. You can have lots of knowledge and be very foolish indeed. Been there, done that! Knowledge is information and facts, while wisdom is knowing how to use and apply them! And let's be honest, experience can teach us a lot about this if we are willing to learn.

I started learning the trombone at age twelve. By the time I was in high school, I was good enough to make all-state band. As an adult, I had the pleasure of sitting in with Maynard Ferguson's Jazz Band when it was on tour in Houston. What a treat for someone who is not a professional musician! These experiences have shown me that over time, I not only learned good trombone techniques but also learned when and how to apply them. Music is more than just having good technique; it is about expressing something. There is no shortcut if you want good trombone playing. Sure, it takes hard work to gain knowledge about good technique, but it takes experience playing and listening to music to develop the wisdom of how to use that hard-won technique.

How do I know that youthfulness has become an idol in America? Because in our dealings with youth we have put their wants, desires, and needs ahead of wisdom. We know that education is important and try to see that our children receive a good one. Think of all the experiences we give our youth outside of school: sports, music, dance, martial arts, and tutoring to name a few. We want our children to have lots of experience as though experience alone can teach wisdom. Yet, we fail to look at what these experiences are teaching our children. There are lots of experiences, lots of youth activities, lots of teaching skills but, unfortunately, little emphasis on developing wisdom. We will have more to say about this later.

Ignoring wisdom is one sign that we idolize our youth because we give children what they want, not what they need. We are actively teaching our children that their feelings have primary importance. But feelings do not provide a good guide to living life. Making feelings primary is a sure recipe for creating a spoiled child. And spoiled children grow up to be spoiled adults. They haven't learned how to be self-governing with any kind of wisdom. Spoiled people insist life must revolve around them and their feelings. Does this remind you of some of the things happening today on college campuses and society at large?

Consider that wisdom requires we be able to think about a problem apart from our current feelings about it. Following our feelings leads to suboptimal results. More and more that is what's happening in our society. Our nation was founded by people who used their reasoning power to understand human nature. The result was their wisdom created a system that gave us freedom.

Do you see the existential threat our youth idolatry has created? We have deemphasized wisdom and exalted feelings.

And youth are often very passionate while lacking in the wisdom needed for channeling and applying that passion. But freedom and prosperity depend on having self-governing people capable of putting feelings and emotions in their proper place. It requires thoughtful people willing to seek and apply wisdom. Our youth culture has been undermining this for decades.

To money and youth idolatry we can add the idol of the celebrity. Undoubtedly, our idolatry of youth and money contributed to the rise of the idol of the celebrity. Let's take a closer look at it now.

Celebrity

Since World War II there have been profound changes in the people that we look to as leaders. One of the big changes is how we let Hollywood celebrities and sports figures influence us. Their opinion is considered important even when it is about areas of which they are essentially ignorant. But celebrity idolatry is bigger than Hollywood and sports stars. It includes the people who become well known through social and traditional medium even if it is only transitory. It may be for a few days, a few weeks, a few months or longer. We respect their authority because we deem their experience authentic.

It's not always wrong to consider what a celebrity person says. But we ought to recognize that being a celebrity does not mean the person has anything relevant or worthwhile to say on the important topics of the day. That requires they study the issues in some depth and think about them before speaking.

Today our idolatry of celebrity people now even extends to groups of people. Think about the scientists that are forecasting climate catastrophe while pushing the green agenda as the solution. Be honest about this. These scientists are treated as infallible and their science as settled. And lots of people are influenced by their views. But have you really looked at the science? Have the people you listen to for guidance really studied the science? Are scientists infallible and their science settled for all time? Of course not!

Perhaps I've just lost your approval because you believe I'm a climate denier. I'm not here to argue one way or the other on this issue. I just want to point out that these climate scientists have obtained celebrity status. And this recognition essentially started because of their predictions of catastrophe. You can see the idolatry because the discussion does not involve any real discussion of the issues or facts. If anything, the discussion is little more than emotional appeals rather than a science discussion.

The problem with idolatry is that it blinds us to the truth. In fact, the truth doesn't matter. Pick your topic of the day and see how little of the discussion is about reality and how much is about emotion. Think gun control, police brutality, campus rape as examples. Our society is becoming unable to discuss such problems in depth and come to a satisfactory resolution. Each side picks its celebrities and listens to their advice. It is understanding and facts that get sacrificed. Where's the wisdom in that?

Before we move on, let's look at one more idol. Our freedom and relative wealth have made it easy for us to have idols in our lives. Arguably the most consequential is how we have made self an idol.

Self

A notable aspect of America in the past on up to today is our emphasis on individuals. This is not inherently a bad thing since we are individuals as well as members of various groups. Indeed, even identical twins that have identical genes are not identical. They are not carbon copies of each other. They are, in fact, unique individuals. Focusing on individuals doesn't make self an idol.

But we fall into idolatry when we insist that reasoning always start with self. Unfortunately, self cannot always provide the proper perspective and give us the answers we need to be successful in life. This is because humans are social creatures. We are, in fact, members of various groups. And group dynamics is something we must consider if we want to maintain proper balance.

Stop and think of all the ways our culture orients you toward yourself. "Have it your way," is one advertising slogan that comes to my mind. I am part of the McDonald's generation.

I expect almost instant gratification. I have gone into McDonald's restaurants where the cash register displays the average serving time for you. This made such an impression on me the first time, I still remember the number: thirty-two seconds! From the time they took my order until I had food in hand, just thirty-two seconds. That's practically instant gratification!

But let me tell you another food story that shows we come into the world with a nature that is naturally oriented toward self. My oldest daughter was small when she was born, was very small as a child, and is still very small. She's so small today she can even wear children's clothes sometimes (and save a lot of money). When she was just under a year old with a vocabulary of a few words, we would put her in her highchair and feed her porridge for breakfast. She would be so hungry that she would cry loudly for breakfast. Would you believe, she would also cry between spoonfuls of porridge, and let me tell you that that tiny girl had a set of lungs! Forget thirty-two seconds. The time it took to get another spoonful of porridge was way too much time! Amazingly, she would eat three full bowls of porridge, which personally I think must have been a miracle. There was no way three bowls of porridge could possibly fit into someone so small. So, our precious daughter, our first-born child did not need to be taught to reference things to herself. When it came to breakfast, it was all about her and getting food. She really was all about instant gratification. My wife and I needn't worry about trying to teach her that skill. She was born with it.

It is quite natural as we grow up to continue to reference everything to ourselves. But as adults, referencing everything to self lacks balance. When we do this, we have made self an idol. We must account for other people because we are social creatures living in a society with other people. In fact, sometimes we need to defer to other people when we would prefer not to. That's called maturity.

Do you remember my story of the pesky stop sign? Consider the driver I know we've all seen. On the highway he is the fastest car, always weaving in and out of traffic trying to get ahead. He never goes the speed limit even on city streets and always tries to get through the yellow light, not always successfully. Apparently, he thinks he owns the road and you are just a nuisance that should get out of his way. Undoubtedly, self is his idol.

As a society, we have not encouraged thoughtful consideration of self-idolatry. Indeed, in many ways we are encouraging it. Consider the push to label things as hate speech. Unfortunately, much of the argument for hate speech is an argument about feelings. I hope you see that feelings can't provide an objective definition for hate speech. Here I'm not arguing that your feelings are wrong. It's just that they can't be the basis for hate speech. Your feelings are yours and only yours. Sure, you can gather other like-minded people and demand change, but that doesn't change the basis of the argument. Each and every person making this argument points to their own feelings. This is making self an idol. It is impossible for another person to know beforehand what will and will not disturb your feelings.

Logically, much of what we say or write can potentially offend someone. Just think of the push to find micro-aggressions. A simple statement like "Make America Great Again" today is being defined as offensive. In the past such a statement would not have been controversial. The difference is that today we are encouraging self-idolatry, which inherently lacks balance.

Societies can't exist with freedom if self-idolatry is the norm. Why? Because then the people in authority will act on the basis of what they want. Since they have the power, they don't need to concern themselves with your thoughts or feelings. Do you really think Hitler was concerned about the thoughts or feelings of the Jews? Self-idolatry left unchecked will always degenerate into tyranny. This is one reason why there is such a push for controlling hate speech in America.

It may not be obvious to you at first, but self-idolatry also has financial consequences. Why do you think there is such a push to forgive all college loan debt? It would certainly be good for every individual with large school debt. But ask yourself a simple question. Why should someone else have to pay for the debt you willing agreed to? Such an idea is essentially a selfish, self-centered viewpoint. It shows self-idolatry.

The biggest financial impact self-idolatry comes about because it destroys our trust in each other. I simply expect you to react to things the way I do. Likewise, you expect me to be predictable because I should be like you. But of course, we're not clones of each other. We're individuals. And when you act contrary to my expectations, it destroys trust between us. I find it more difficult to trust you and trust is our next topic.

Trust

So far, we have focused on how Americans feel entitled, presuming our good fortune will continue. We presume either through ignorance or self-deception; either brings negative consequences. Many of our current problems are a direct result of our choices, which are too often motivated by idolatry. We routinely violate the laws of economics and even the laws of nature. We should characterize this as wickedness.

When we violate the principles of our universe, we naturally reap the consequences. There is nothing mysterious or supernatural about this. But make no mistake, judgment does come when wickedness abounds. Why? Because reality can only be ignored for a time, but not forever!

I think it is safe to say that we are already experiencing the initial stages of the breakdown of our society as a natural consequence of turning to our own way, lusting after money and the power money brings. Or perhaps more likely, lusting after power and then making the system reward us financially. That's what the elite in America seem to have done since 1971. That topic's worthy of a book itself. However, in this chapter I want to start looking at how reality can bring judgment against America. Let's see how it's a natural consequence of our actions.

I have purposefully entitled this chapter "Trust" because at the foundation of our society, what is being destroyed in America is trust. It may not have ever occurred to you to think about the US dollar and its value in the world as a measure of the trust our society has at any given point in time. But this is so. Consequently, we must look at the connection between money and trust. Let's do this by looking at a simple example.

This week, Texas rancher Bubba Brown took the fruits of his labor to market: his Angus beef cows. Let me assure you that Bubba worked really hard to nurture and grow those guys big and fat so you and I could enjoy our favorite steaks. Now, in years gone by and still in some places in the world, Bubba would barter with someone to get the clothes he needs. Then he would barter with someone else to get the tools and supplies he needs for his ranch. All this takes time and energy away from raising those wonderful Angus beef cows we want to enjoy. But despite Bubba's name, he is really sharp intellectually and knows how to save time and become more productive. Instead of bartering, Bubba sells his wonderful Angus beef cows for money. Since Bubba is sharp, he gets what he considers a fair price. The money he accepts he believes is a fair measure of his time and effort. So now, Bubba has money to spend in the form of cash in his pocket.

But wait. Bubba just has some pieces of rather nice, sturdy paper printed with green ink in his pocket. Intrinsically, it only has value worth a fraction of a cent. I suppose he could use it to write his shopping list on or maybe start a fire with it. What really makes his particular green paper valuable is that Bubba absolutely trusts that he can take it to someone else and they will accept it for payment. Implicitly, that person trusts the money is a proper measure of Bubba's time and effort. Without trust on the part of both people, the paper bills are essentially worthless. In that case Bubba might as well burn his money for heat and at least get some use out of it.

Let's not stop there. Let's follow the money another step. Bubba is a conservative sort of person, so he takes his money and puts it in the bank for safekeeping. Again, Bubba must have trust for a second time. He trusts that the bank will always keep his money safe and let him spend it as needed. Of course, the bank accumulates lots of cash from all the Bubbas of the region. Down the road, Bubba's neighbor, Farmer Jones, decides to expand his operations to make more money. He needs a new barn, which will help him make more money year after year. Unfortunately, Farmer Jones doesn't have enough cash to build his barn. Like his neighbor Bubba, Farmer Jones is also a really smart businessman. He decides to go where there is a ready pile of cash. He goes to the bank. There he takes out a loan, gets the money he needs, and pays Big Al to build the barn.

Scenarios like this happen every day throughout America. But it can only happen if there is trust. The bank must trust that Farmer Jones will repay the loan with interest, so the bank makes some money for all its efforts. Any loan requires trust, otherwise it is just a gift. But let's think some more about the bank. Because the bank made a loan, it no longer has all the money it took in from all the Bubbas. This means the bank must have additional trust in all its customers. The bank must trust their customers won't ask for all their money all at once. And all the customers must have enough trust in the bank to feel secure or they will ask! They need to trust the bank will not go out of business and take their money with it. Otherwise, there is a run on the bank, which has happened many times before.

America, being so clever, created the Federal Deposit Insurance Corporation to reassure the bank's customers that their trust was well placed. The federal government would pay if the bank couldn't. More trust needed! Everything seems fine unless the government runs out of money to pay the bank customers when the bank fails. Is there a problem here? We can't give a proper answer without looking at value, which we discuss in the next chapter. Suffice it to say that without trust, the paper money has no value.

It is important for you to see that at the very foundation of an economic system based on money is trust. Without trust the system can't work. Since each transaction using money involves at least some trust, it is reasonable to say that the total value of the commerce in a society is in some sense a measure of the trust in that society. One way we can measure this commerce is called the gross domestic product or GDP. In the recent past, we have seen America's GDP go down. We call a prolonged downturn a recession. When we take a closer look during a recession at the banks and Bubbas of America, we see that less money is changing hands. Both the banks and individuals are holding onto their money longer in order to reduce risk. They reduce risk by not extending as much trust to others.

Now let's focus on just one part of the economy to see what happens as trust evaporates and people, banks, and other businesses start holding onto their money. Let's look at housing. During 2009, did housing prices in your area of the country go up or down? In most places, 2009 was not a good year for housing. Unfortunately, 2010 really wasn't much better. Overall, housing prices declined, in some places 25% or more. We call this the result of supply and demand. There were too many houses on the market for the number of people able and willing to buy. If you were someone who owned a home during this time, you saw the value of your home decline. And your overall wealth decreased. But at the foundation of this supply and demand dynamic is trust. As trust decreased in America, there was a decrease in economic activity. Essentially, the banks and mortgage companies lost trust in the customer's ability to pay back the loans. They made it more difficult to get a mortgage loan (less trust) and the demand for housing collapsed. Hence, the decline in housing prices we experienced.

I want to be perfectly clear and make sure you understand this. When trust decreases or is destroyed, then wealth is destroyed. With less trust there is less value so wealth disappears. It is really that simple. In recent years America has gone through several episodes of decreased trust. Just think about the dot.com crisis and the more recent housing crisis. These are definite signs that trust or the lack of it has become a significant issue for us as a nation. We are experiencing the natural consequences of doing things our own way rather than looking at and understanding reality. The truth is we need to understand more about trust and more about value if we want to resolve our problems.

Please do not get confused. Here we are not talking about trust in oneself. As long as I am alive, I trust myself to breathe. I trust myself to eat. I trust I will get out of bed in the morning. That trust is a given. What we are really talking about is trust between each other as individuals and as various organizations (government, companies, and other organizations). This is the kind of trust that directly affects our wellbeing but is not under our complete control. Consider this: the mortgage company also trusts I will get out of bed in the morning, but their trust goes beyond that. They trust I will go to work and earn the money to pay for the loan. Their trust doesn't last very long if I get behind on my payments!

Based on the performance of America's economy and its overwhelming and rapidly increasing debt, I can safely say America as a society has lost sight of the necessity for trust. America is very much in danger of finding itself on a death walk. There is no promise, no guarantee that we will always exist as a prosperous nation or a nation at all. As a nation we can certainly walk a path leading to oblivion. And we can walk a path that ultimately destroys the dollar. And quite frankly, that certainly seems to be what we are choosing to do.

I know that economics is much more complicated than I have portrayed it here. We could go into much more depth and look at all sorts of statistics. We could even do comparisons between economies of different cultures to see who really is performing best. But this would just obscure the fact that trust is essential for economies to work properly. And trust is at the heart of America's economic problems. We are rapidly becoming a nation that is less and less trustful and our dollar is leading the way. We can only trust in the dollar if we can trust other people, including our government.

Make no mistake about this. The government is an organization of people made by people. We have vested the authority to make money solely in government. But we are not talking about something abstract. We are talking about people: policy makers, regulators and enforcers, and anonymous people in Treasury and other relevant parts of government. These are the people we must trust to take care of our American currency. And that means they must take care of your money and my money. Or they should. And that's the problem today. Are they really taking care of our currency?

There is an inherent problem with trust. Humans are willing to extend trust based on experience. If the experience has been positive, then the next time, we are more willing to extend trust. But the opposite is also true. If our experience has been negative, then the next time we are less willing to extend trust. This means positive trends reinforce more positive trends, but negative trends reinforce more negative trends.

Apply this to the dollar. As long as the financial system experiences positive trends, then this tends to reinforce itself, so the future is also positive. But when the economy experiences a negative trend, it reinforces the negative trend making a negative future more likely. The government naturally tries to intervene to stop negative trends from reinforcing themselves. But what happens if we lose faith in the government's ability or desire to stop negative trends? That's fundamentally an issue of trust.

In this chapter we have focused on trust because it is so fundamental to any sound financial system. Without trust, value is destroyed. And money must have value in order to be useful! This is logical and makes sense. But it assumes we really understand money and value. You may be surprised to learn that money and value are not really understood well by people, even some very educated people. This is just another problem our society has that can have very negative consequences. For this reason, money and value are the topics for the next two chapters. Remember, ignorance doesn't protect us from reality!

Money

In the last chapter we focused on trust because it is the foundation upon which financial systems arc built. The chapter finished with an obvious conclusion. The dollar can only be as strong as the trust people have in the dollar. Hopefully, you can understand why this must be so. In this chapter we need to look more closely at the dollar itself. Why? Because you and I think of dollars as money, but this is not so. And this makes us vulnerable to the quick change reality can bring.

Fundamentally, we don't understand the meaning of money. If I ask you how much money you have, you can count the dollars in your pockets and give me an answer. But maybe this doesn't satisfy you. You remind me that you have money in your checking and savings accounts. Fine, add those into your calculations. Is that how much money you have? What about the CD's you have at the bank? Did you count those dollars? Now you're satisfied!

We should both be happy that now we agree on how much money you have. Yet, there is something not quite right. If you count the money in your CD's, then why not count the money in your stocks and bonds? They're not much different than CDs. They can be sold and converted to dollars, which proves they must be money like CDs. And I bet you forgot to add in the dollars you have in travelers checks left over from your vacation.

Notice in trying to define money we included physical dollars, dollars in our checking and savings accounts, CDs, stocks, bonds, and travelers checks and that's not an exhaustive list. Maybe you think the government must know how much money is in the economy. But they have the same problem we just encountered. Their solution is to have four basic measures (plus several others) for estimating money supply:

- M0 = the physical notes and coins

- M1 = M0 + demand deposits, checking type accounts, and travelers checks
- M2 = M1 + savings accounts, money market accounts, mutual funds, CDs under $100,000
- M3 = M2 + all other large time deposits

Even the federal government doesn't seem to have a clear understanding of money. That's why they have multiple definitions for defining money. The reality is that you and I and the government don't appreciate that money must have a single definition. Intuitively we know this. That's why we so easily say that dollars are money. But as we tried to count how much money we had, we quickly discovered it must include items other than physical dollar bills and coins. We came up with a list of things to include in our calculation. And we discovered the US government has even more measures for the money supply. But this can only mean we don't understand the essence of money.

This may shock you, but none of the things we included in our list for counting our own money is actually money! I can hear your objections now. "Of course, my dollars are money. I spend it at various stores all the time!"

This certainly seems to make sense. And that's how I normally think about money too. Unfortunately, our thinking and understanding is clouded by our emotions. We are simply too close to the situation. Quite frankly, I depend on the dollars I have in my wallet and in the bank to carry on in my life. I really have a hard time believing this is not money. Do you sympathize with me on this?

Remember, the tipoff that we have a problem in our understanding is there is no clear definition for money. So, let's eliminate our emotional attachment to the dollar by looking back in history at the denarius. This was a small silver coin of the Roman Empire in use from approximately 200 B.C. to 250 A.D.

From its beginning until the first century A.D., the denarius was about 3.9 grams (the weight of two dimes) and was 95-98% silver. It was widely accepted and widely used. It worked well as money for many years.

During the last two hundred years of its life as money, it was repeatedly devalued. First, it was reduced in weight. Then the silver content was repeatedly reduced until ultimately the denarius was 50% or less silver. Not surprisingly, the result was the coin lost value. Why? Because it had less and less silver.

Does that give you a clue about money? It should. It shows the value of the denarius wasn't in the denarius as a coin. It was in the silver the denarius contained. Less silver equals less value. The denarius was just a convenient way to package the silver because it was a standard. And this was still true when the Romans made it a smaller coin with less silver content. It represented a standard for silver that people could trust.

Apply this thinking to the dollar. Today, what standard does the dollar depend on? It's not gold because there's no gold in the dollar bills or backing the bills. Since August 15, 1971, we don't have the right to get a fixed gold amount in exchange for our dollars. The dollar price of gold has fluctuated ever since. The denarius had inherent value because of the silver in it. But what's the real value of my one-dollar bill today? Like the denarius coin, it's not the dollar bill that has the value. Unlike the denarius, there is no gold or silver backing the dollar. The obvious conclusion is the dollar represents the trust we have in the dollar. Or if you prefer, trust in the government which says the dollar is backed by the full faith and trust of the US government. But trust can be destroyed.

It's hard to take dollars seriously as money if it only represents trust. I would much prefer dollars to have something of value they represent. The thought of it being just paper does not warm my heart! Really, I'm just saying I'd like my money to have real value, not just trust. We will talk about value in the next chapter because money and value must be related. Before we do that, let's look at one more problem in our understanding of money.

If my dollar bills don't represent money, then I suppose my checking and savings accounts don't represent money either. That's a disturbing thought! Can I make this clear to you? If my checking and savings account aren't money, then what are they? They are actually loans to the bank for which the bank provides services in lieu of interest payments. And the bank very cleverly sends out monthly statement showing how much money you have in the bank. Those statements are only fancy IOUs. The bank is telling you how much money they owe you! They are not telling you how much money you physically have in the bank.

When you deposited your money in the bank, I'm sure you didn't realize you made a loan to the bank. Remember Bubba and Farmer Jones? The bank took your money and loaned it out in hopes of making enough money to pay its debt to you. Sometimes they can't. When a bank fails, it can't pay all its debts so what happens to your "money." The government only guarantees to pay up to $250,000 when the bank can't pay. After that, you are treated like any other creditor. All this time you thought you had money in the bank. Instead, what you had was a promise from the bank to pay you back. You didn't recognize it, but you were extending trust to the bank. So, we're back to seeing that trust is fundamental to any system of money.

I hope you now see the confusion that exists about money. We think our paper money is real money. We think our checking and savings accounts hold our money. But what we have is pretty, green paper and IOUs from the bank! The denarius always had value because of the silver content and people always value silver. But what does this tell us about the inherent value any of the things we think of as money? If there's little or no real underlying value, then what prevents the collapse of our money? The answer is only trust itself and this has a habit of wearing out. History teaches us that currency can only last if it represents something of real value. Gold and silver always have value because people throughout history have always valued gold and silver. That's what gives money it's value. To understand this, we need to understand value and that's the topic of the next chapter.

Value

We've already seen that the dollar went off the gold standard in 1971. Since then, the value of the dollar has depended solely on trust. Fundamentally, there is a built-in temptation for government to simply print more money when it needs it. But the law of supply and demand still holds true. The government can and does add money faster than goods and services grow. The result is inflation. At low levels we tolerate it. But inflation actual represents a transfer of wealth from us to the government. Each of our dollars is worth a little bit less and all that missing wealth is found in the newly printed money of the government. And most people don't understand the theft that is happening. That doesn't sound like a trust building exercise.

Look at any US paper money and it says, "This note is legal tender for all debts, public and private." We depend on (i.e., trust) this to be so in order to continue doing business. However, you need to understand that before August 15, 1971 you could redeem your dollar for gold. Since then, the dollar has not been tied to anything that has real value. In effect, my dollar is just a piece of paper with nice green ink and an elaborate design. We call this fiat money because more money can be created by fiat (authoritative order of the government). History shows us that fiat money always ends up with no value for the simple reason that it destroys all the underlying trust. Unlike the denarius that had value from the silver, fiat money has nothing of value behind it. Fiat money works so long as people have trust in it. But what happens when people start questioning the value of the money? To fully understand this, we need to make sure we understand value.

Let's revisit Bubba and his wonderful Angus beef. If I'm hungry, then Bubba's beef has value to me. Not surprisingly, the hungrier I am, the more value Bubba's beef has to me. Don't get confused. I am not talking about supply and demand directly. Instead, I am talking about need. It is need that defines the value something has for me. If I am adrift for days in a small boat on the ocean and without any water, a one-hundred-dollar bill has no value to me. I would gladly trade one hundred dollars for a quart of drinkable water. Reverse the scenario. I'm in a boat with plenty of food and water. Will I pay one hundred dollars to get an extra quart of water? Of course not! If I already have plenty of water, an extra quart of water has no value to me. My need directly defines the value of something for me.

When people start questioning the value of a dollar, they are questioning its ability to satisfy our needs. I'm more than willing to exchange my time and effort (my work) for some of Bubba's wonderful beef. But neither Bubba nor I want to barter my services for his beef. Instead, we want something, called money, that represents a standard of measuring the value of our respective work. Our work has value so the money we exchange must have value. And it must hold this value reasonably well or both of us will start to question the value of the money we are trying to exchange. Do you see what can happen? He and I can decide there is too little value in the dollars we want to exchange. At that point, the money no longer fits our need. We become like the person dying of thirst floating on the ocean. Dollar bills are no use to such a person, so they have no value. Likewise, Bubba and I can decide dollars are untrustworthy, so dollars cease to have any value for us. Multiply this to everyone in America in a chain reaction. That's a catastrophe.

The one thing that can prevent the catastrophe we just outlined is if the money Bubba and I want to exchange always has some inherent value. History shows us that gold and silver, especially gold, have always been desired by men. From ancient times until today gold and silver have been valued. People want it and it is always relatively scarce. That's why the denarius always had value. It never completely lost its value through devaluation (removing some silver content). There was always some silver in it. The silver gave the denarius inherent value.

I hope it's obvious that for something to have and maintain value, it must be consistently desired and must also be scarce. It can't be plentiful or easy to find or it would lose its value. This is exactly what happened to salt. Perhaps you know our word salary comes from the Latin word for salt. During the Roman Empire soldiers were often paid with salt. It was scarce and people wanted it, so it had real value. When salt became plentiful and easy to find, it no longer was used as money. Why? Because it had lost its value.

Since August1971, the dollar has lost 70-75% of its value. This is a direct result of not being tied to anything of real, lasting value. The average American didn't understand the significance of this change when it happened because they assumed the dollar was real money. It's logical to say a dollar today was a dollar yesterday and will be tomorrow, but this is only true if there is inherent value in the dollar. The government did away with the gold standard, which let them print the money they needed. The dollars you have today have much less value than the dollars you put in your savings account in 1971. The government has appropriated some (most) of the value in the intervening years.

Sadly, the government hasn't been content to just appropriate the value of your money without any compensation. The government has also figured out how to steal value from the future. They do this by borrowing money. We saw that borrowing requires trust that the loan will be repaid in the future. But the government has borrowed far more than it can possibly pay back. This guarantees that the government must appropriate more of the value of your money to pay off the debt.

Do you see how precarious a situation we are in? The government is now in the position of having to effectively steal value from your money for the foreseeable future. The end result of this is that trust in the dollar is destroyed. Eventually it will no longer have enough value to be useful. That will be a catastrophe.

If government can steal value from our money, then it must mean the government has the power necessary to steal that value. Thus, we need to understand power, which is our next topic.

Power

America has such a large economy that it must have built up a lot of trust over the decades. Certainly, the American people must have been doing something right. But our increasing economic problems in the last few decades clearly show that we have somehow gotten off the path. Trust has been and continues to be undermined and eroded. How and why does this happen?

Studies have shown that increasing the amount of money a person or family has increases happiness and satisfaction only up to a point. Once that point is reached, increased money tends to be correlated with less happiness and satisfaction with life, not more. Can you guess where that magical point is in America (and probably everywhere else too)? That special point is where a person or family has enough money to pay for basic food, clothing, and shelter without the constant worry of where the next meal is coming from or how to make the mortgage or rent payment. They are essentially free of the worry of being homeless and not being able to provide adequate food and clothing. In short, they are no longer concerned with trying to provide the basic necessities of life. It is not a minute-by-minute or hour-by-hour struggle to make ends meet like it is for the poor and near poor. This point can be reached in America in what we would call the lower middle class in rural areas and towns. In cities it is usually middle to upper middle class. This is the vast majority of Americans. So why is it so many people strive so hard to get more money? Why would billionaires like Warren Buffett or Bill Gates even need to work? Or consider the less rich. Do the Wall Street workers getting multi-million-dollar annual bonuses really need to go back for more? They all could stop working and spend the rest of their lives pursuing a myriad of other interests. So why don't they? What keeps them working to get even more money? The answer cannot be that they need the money. No, it is not the money they want or need; it is the power that comes with the money.

Power is very seductive. Can you imagine walking into the grocery store without the least concern for cost? You only need to decide what nice, delectable thing you want for dinner right now. Cost? Who cares! Kobe beef from Japan? Why not? That's power over your life. What about your car? How old is it? Is it paid for yet? Imagine walking into any auto dealer tomorrow and telling the salesman you want to buy a car with all the upgrades for cash. I guarantee that you will get excellent service! That's power over the salesman's life. Now his life is revolving around your wants and desires. Need I go on? In short, we say, "money talks!"

Let's go back and look at Bubba again as he goes to sell those wonderful Angus beef cows. He wants to get a fair price for his labor. What he would like is for the buyer and himself to come to an agreement about this fair price. If the buyer also has it in mind to arrive at a fair price, then there is a good chance they will come to an agreement that is good for both of them. But suppose the buyer really wants the power that more money brings. Now he has an incentive to take advantage of Bubba instead of settling for a fair price. Remember, Bubba is not stupid; he's sharp. He quickly realizes the buyer doesn't really want to be fair. What happens to Bubba's trust in this buyer? It certainly doesn't increase. But let's be honest. Adults generally are aware of and consider that a buyer, salesman, or service person has a real incentive to maximize his own benefits at their expense. Bubba can still deal with the buyer as long as the negotiations on pricing come out close to being fair.

The problem for Bubba and you and I is that someone like Bernie Madoff comes along. All the transactions over all the years that were made with Madoff's investment company seemed beneficial to the investors. Right up to the time the Ponzi scheme crashed. Suddenly, without warning, all that apparent wealth disappeared. It only existed on paper, not in reality. The power Bernie Madoff craved overrode any sense of fair play. Ultimately, Madoff wanted money without returning any real value, so he found a way to simply take it. That's an exercise in power, power over other people and their money, which gave him more power to control his own life.

After Madoff, is it so hard to imagine that a potential investor must wonder if his investment will really be safe or if it will magically disappear? This is a much bigger problem than having enough trust to negotiate a fair value for an investment. It really raises the question if any transaction can ever be made safely. Society recognizes this as a fundamental problem to the economic system and passes laws against this kind of greed. But remember, behind the greed is the desire for power, the power to control, the power to take from someone else without giving value in return, the power to live a lavish lifestyle. There is a thirst for the power to do whatever you want in your own life. Money is just the means to this end.

Recall that I said humans are prone sometimes to choose evil. More often rather than choosing evil, we simply choose a less than optimal way for the simple reason that it's not always easy to tell which way the right way is. Much of life seems to require us to choose the way that seems best to us. It's only as we experience the consequence that we learn how good a choice we made.

This all makes sense until we consider how power corrupts. If I choose the way that seems best to me, then I must think it is the right way. But my actions do affect other people either positively or negatively. And the more power I have, the more likely my actions affect more people. Since I am sure I choose the "best" way, I can easily excuse negative consequences, especially if they only affect other people.

Do you think Bernie Madoff was simply ignorant and didn't understand that a Ponzi scheme cannot ultimately last? Of course not! He knew his scheme would unravel sometime. He even thought several times that he was about to be caught when he was investigated by the Securities and Exchange Commission. But until then, he was determined to live the "good life." He knew to do good but desired power more, the power more money would bring. And his actions destroyed trust and undermined the very system that generated his wealth in the first place.

But you say you are not like Bernie Madoff. You are not a crook or swindler. Yet the issue before us is this: do you want power, the power to exercise more control over your life? I am sure you do. Bernie Madoff went about making his choices so he could live in a big mansion, take wonderful vacations, and have nice things. His money gave him power. Your money gives you power. But I must point out that it is not inherently evil to have money and the power money brings. However, we must guard against misusing our power to live only for self (self-idolatry again). Bernie Madoff was focused primarily on himself and only secondarily on his family, although the reality was that he was hurting his family just like an invisible cancer before it is discovered. How much like Bernie Madoff are you in this way? You say, "Not at all!" I certainly hope so.

Over the years, as America became richer and more powerful, its citizens became more selfish. Like Bernie Madoff, they used their wealth and power to live the good life. They wanted more things, nicer cars, and bigger houses. In 1970, the average home size was just 1400 square feet. By 2004, this had expanded to 2330 square feet, a 2/3 increase in size in thirty-four years. Not content to spend their own money, Americans found a way to borrow large sums personally. Still not being content, they decided to take money from other people just like Bernie Madoff, only legally. That's a large part of what government does today, redistributes money. Americans even found a way to steal from their own children! We call this increasing the national debt. We spend the money, but our children must pay it back! Never before in American history have so many people gone so far in debt either in absolute terms or as a percentage of income. And we force our children into debt so we won't have to pay it all ourselves. At its heart this is simply an exercise in power.

I am tempted to say our wealth and the power it brought corrupted us. But this is not really the case. Our human nature is already prone to temptation. The money and power only allowed us to demonstrate this fact. We have been seduced by the desire to have more power over our lives. Today husbands and wives frequently both work hard to earn more money so they can exercise more power to do exactly what Bernie Madoff wanted to do – live a more luxurious lifestyle, the good life. We have not been as bad as Bernie Madoff, but we have failed to see how our preferred lifestyle exercises power to destroy trust.

In your life and my life, the day-to-day and minute-to-minute question that is always being answered is, "what kind of person will we be?" The truth is, we can be selfish or caring of others. Bernie Madoff accumulated money and its power but forgot something really important to life: family, friends, and other people.

I don't think the people with power set out to destroy trust. But the desire for more money and more power has led to more and more actions where value is not being given and received equitably. Remember Bubba and I can only continue to do business if we think there is an equitable distribution of value. If I start using my power to Bubba's detriment, then at some point Bubba will lose trust in my honesty and will stop trading with me. That's the end result of abusing my power.

It is important we remember that power corrupts us by letting us be more self-centered. And self-centered people elect a self-serving government. What's the outcome? Power is used inappropriately, and trust is destroyed. And that is what has been happening in America for many years now. This cannot end well unless we decide to change.

Pt II: Stormy Weather

Breaking Storm

In the previous section we looked at some of the reasons behind America going astray. The accumulative effect of all of these means a major correction must occur. We can't know the exact timing or the exact form of the correction, but we know that adverse trends cannot continue to build forever. Anything that can't go on forever won't!

It is possible that correction could become very bloody. We know the United States experienced a civil war in order to resolve the issue of slavery. It cost the lives of an estimated 620,000 men or about 2% of the US population. A similar conflict today would cost 6,600,000 lives. While armed conflict is theoretically possible, there have been several significant events that point to a much more likely financial correction. Examples are the dotcom bust and more recently the housing market collapse leading to an almost catastrophic financial market failure.

In this section we will focus on instability cascades usually inherent in complex systems such as the financial system. It is this cascade vulnerability that makes a catastrophe possible. Think for a moment about earthquakes. They remain unpredictable and can be very catastrophic. But scientists tell us there are usually signs that an earthquake is becoming imminent. Seismometers measuring vibrations in the earth detect increases in very small earthquakes. Hydrologists sometimes notice changes in ground water flow, and satellites measure changes in ground height. Scientist can even measure the increasing strain on the rocks. In the same way a financial catastrophe sends out signals before it occurs. We only need to look carefully and observe the signs and believe their warning!

At the end of this section we will look at one possible scenario of how judgment will come to America. It is not presented as an accurate picture of coming events. Rather, it is a way to let you understand how a financial catastrophe can affect your day to day life. Hopefully, it will wake you up to the possibility that just because something catastrophic hasn't happened in your lifetime means it won't happen. And that means there is still hope. A catastrophe is not inevitable. The trends are clear. The precursor warnings have been happening. Tick, tock, tick, tock. Time is running out. We just need to decide to use our remaining time wisely. The choice is ours to make.

Complexity

In the very first chapter we talked about the good outweighing the bad in a complex system. We noted that this was a misleading way to look at such systems. We used the human body as an example. I can lose an arm or a leg and still lead a productive, fulfilling life. If my heart stops, I'm dead even if every other part of my body functions perfectly. That's an inherent property of many complex systems, including our economy.

Here I'd like to suggest we look more closely at the human body to see what more we can learn about complex systems. Think about a heart attack for a moment. It is the final result of a malfunctioning system. The malfunction didn't start as a big problem, the heart attack. It started as a little buildup of plaque in the arteries. The buildup was so small it wasn't noticeable at all. Only specialized equipment could detect the problem. The body didn't notice; it worked just fine.

At some point a piece of plaque breaks loose. It can happen when there's only a little plaque or a lot of plaque. It is an inherently unpredictable event but can be catastrophic whichever it is. This tells us complex systems can fail unpredictably from a very little trigger event. Perhaps you want another example to see this problem clearly.

Do you remember hearing about the butterfly effect? A butterfly flaps its wings in Africa and America gets a hurricane. Or maybe you heard some variation of this story. It points out the very problem that makes weather forecasts for next week so unreliable. Very small changes in temperature, pressure, humidity, winds, etc. in a little area can grow into a major weather event. We just can't measure all these small changes.

I live in Houston and it's quite common in summer for weather reports to track small weather patterns coming off the coast of Africa. With the right conditions these can form thunderstorms that grow until the wind patterns start rotating.

Over warm water the wind circulation grows in speed and size until it becomes a hurricane. The small event leaving Africa becomes a major event in the Caribbean Ocean. But it is impossible to predict if a hurricane will form when the weather first leaves Africa heading for the Americas.

Weather is an interesting complex system for a lot of reasons. One is simply that we live in it. But it also suggests that we can get better weather forecasts by measuring the current weather in more detail. This is certainly true but only incrementally true. There is always something happening that we don't or can't measure that becomes a major weather pattern. Think about the progress meteorologists have made in the last fifty years. Weather forecasts are pretty good twenty-four hours ahead. They are some help two days ahead. I doubt you are very surprised when the weather forecast for three days ahead turns out to be wrong.

Sometimes the weather forms a strong pattern that is not easily changed. When this happens, the meteorologists can more reliably predict the weather three and four days ahead. I hope you see the reason. Small variations in temperature, pressure, humidity, etc. can't grow very well because the weather pattern is so strong. But we should not be lulled into thinking weather forecasting has gotten so much better. The weather will change, and it will become more unpredictable again.

Now let's take what we have just learned and apply it to our economy. Money flows through the economy as people go about their business. This is like our own body's blood flow. If either stops or decreases significantly, a collapse can happen depending on where it occurred in the system. A blood clot in the leg is certainly painful but not necessarily life threatening. If you can't pay your bills and declare bankruptcy, this would be personally painful. It probably won't wreak the economy. But if one of our small financial institutions has a problem, it can be the equivalent of our heart when the plaque decreases or stops the blood flow. The small financial institution can't pay its bills. The money flow has stopped and starts a cascade of bad events just like in a heart attack.

This is what happened in our last financial crisis. Money stopped flowing among financial systems because a small financial institution couldn't pay its bills. This started a cascade of bad events. If the small company couldn't pay its bills, then maybe bigger companies doing the same thing wouldn't be able to pay their bills in the future. Trust was destroyed with the predictable result that financial institutions started holding onto their money. The money flow rapidly decreased. We essentially had a financial heart attack. It was only through quick intervention that the system recovered. And that's true for a real heart attack too. Rapid intervention can prevent a lot of permanent damage. But prevention is even better!

Both the human body and the weather show us how a small event can cause a cascade of events that lead to catastrophe. Let's call this a vulnerability cascade. Both our body and our economy have many potential vulnerability cascades. We are a long way from knowing all the ways events can cascade to catastrophe. This tells us complexity can surprise us in unexpected and unfortunate ways. It tells us catastrophe can happen because of very small, minor trigger events.

This is certainly true, but doesn't give the whole story. Sometimes we do understand vulnerability cascades. That's why I take medicine to lower my cholesterol. I reduce the risk of a trigger event causing a vulnerability cascade that kills me. That's a good example from medicine.

In the next chapter, I'd like to show you a vulnerability cascade we do understand in our economic system. Because we understand it, we may be able to prevent it from happening. But if it is triggered, it will result in the destruction of the dollar, the very dollars we think of as money.

Destroying the Dollar

We have previously seen that the way an economy can be destroyed is by destroying trust. Economies only work based on trust. That is why I have said that in some sense the size of our gross domestic product (GDP) is a measure of the total trust in our society. Another way to examine this is to simply look at the value of the dollar. As Americans have turned away from virtue, from doing what is right, more and more of the real value of our dollar has been destroyed. Indeed, since 1913 when the Federal Reserve was founded in part to protect the value of the dollar, the dollar has lost 96% of its purchasing power. It should come as no surprise to learn that much of this loss came since 1971.

When I first learned that the dollar had lost 96% of its value over the last century, my reaction was that the dollar had pretty much become worthless. But a little reflection led me to realize this is not at all the case. We have only to look at how our economy has grown over the last century to realize the dollar could not be worthless. The 4% value the dollar has retained means we have been able to continue as though nothing has been wrong. But we are rapidly approaching the point where the 4% value will rapidly lose all value bringing economic hardship worse than the Great Depression.

One of our problems as Americans seems to be our narrow thinking. For instance, we know a society cannot tolerate measurements that change. A foot or a pound must be a specific foot and pound for everyone. We take this for granted. But we tend to overlook the deeper meaning of this.

I know when I go to buy (sometimes expensive, sometimes cheap) gasoline, I will get a full gallon when I pump one gallon. In fact, there is a sticker on the pump stating when it was last calibrated for accuracy. Really, it never occurs to me to worry about being cheated. My conclusion could easily be that differing measures is a non-issue here in America. But this is so only if we consider the most specific applications of differing measures. As I said, we need to think deeper so we understand the principle behind rules and laws against differing measures.

Someone who is using differing weights and measures depending on whether they are buying or selling something is trying to gain an unfair advantage and is defrauding the customer. It is no different in its essence than what Bernie Madoff did. He got something without returning the value implied by the transaction. It is a form of stealing. We need to recognize the deeper principle behind the prohibition against differing weights and measures. It is all about giving and getting value, and this has a much broader application than the volume of a gallon of gasoline.

Let me ask you a simple question. If the Federal Reserve is tasked with protecting the value of the dollar, do you think a 96% loss in value in a century qualifies as protecting the dollar? I certainly don't. So why as Americans have we allowed this to occur without a huge outcry? Our actions with respect to the dollar suggest we are not at all concerned with its value. We have been like sheep being led to slaughter. We have gone meekly along without any complaint or protest. And how has this happened to us? What narcotic has dulled us to the truth? It has been the narcotic of low inflation that has dulled us to what has been happening. Low inflation gives the illusion that our economy is really growing and we are prospering when, in fact, part of the apparent growth is not growth at all. It is a loss of value in the dollar.

I can give you an example from my own life. When I finally got my geophysics degree in 1978, I went to work for a starting salary of $19,600/year. As you would expect, it did not stay that low for very long. Every year I got a nice pay raise and some years saw more than one. If I got a pay raise of two or three hundred dollars per month, I never once said to myself, "How much of this pay raise is real and how much is due to inflation?" No, I said "Now I can pay back the car loan much easier!" I was very happy to get the extra money. But think about that car loan for a moment. I was paying it back with dollars that had lost value. They were no longer truly equal to the dollars I borrowed. If you will, I was using a different measure for the value of the dollar. The only reason the bank didn't object is that they already knew I was going to do this so they required I pay back more dollars than I would have if the dollar were stable in value. Both the bank and I agreed to this system of differing measures. While the bank and I may agree to do business this way, it does not suspend the laws of economics. A deeper understand requires we look at the underlying value of the exchange. Unfortunately, inflation was blinding me to the actual value of the transaction of borrowing and paying off the loan. That's the fundamental problem of differing measures. It hides the true value of the transaction from me. And it makes it possible for others to steal from me without my knowledge. Does this seem too harsh? Or maybe too impractical? Let me assure you, the laws of economics are very practical, it's how economies actually work.

I do not think for a moment that as Americans we could stop society from wanting a modest amount of inflation. It is just too enticing and does such a nice job of hiding the truth. But truth is truth. By 2015 a geophysicist coming out of college would start at about $80,000/year. It took four times my starting salary to hire a geophysicist! This implies that the dollar had lost 75% of its value in those thirty years. And all along the way I was happily getting pay raises that were in part illusion because value was being destroyed by inflation.

The alternative to modest inflation is to allow for periods of mild deflation. But unlike inflation, deflation does not mask the truth. We feel the pain immediately. We won't get a pay raise and may even be asked to take a pay cut. Or worse, we may be laid off as fewer workers are needed to fill the shrinking demand for goods and services. The value of our house, our pension, our investments all decrease. And as humans we make things worse because we hold onto the dollars we might otherwise spend since we are afraid of what might happen to us in the future. The economy contracts further and the danger is that the economy collapses into a depression because of a vicious feedback cycle of less spending, further contraction, and further penny pinching on our part. Low inflation seems like a much better alternative to protect us from the danger of a collapsing economy! And low inflation looks so much better and makes us think things are getting better when, in fact, they may be getting worse.

Fundamentally, the way to create low inflation is to create slightly more money than the actual value of the total goods and services available. This tends to cause prices to rise to sop up all those extra dollars. But this can only mean that each dollar now has less value since the total real value didn't change. Do you see the problem? I still buy a gallon of gas and food at the grocery store but overlook the real value underlying these transactions.

Just because something looks good, doesn't mean that it is. Generally, humans succumb and embrace something that looks good, even when it's inherently bad. Especially when it has the narcotic effect of making us feel good and think everything is okay, like low inflation! But Americans need to be more perceptive and smarter than to fall into this trap.

The thinking that has led to our current financial situation is really based on the thinking that some inflation is good because the alternative is deflation. Unfortunately, inflation tends to create bubbles when the extra available dollars start moving toward one area such as housing. The dollars chasing housing causes the price of housing to increase well beyond the actual underlying value of the housing. Remember, anything not based in reality cannot go on forever. The bubble of ever-increasing housing prices not based on a real increase in value must burst at some time. Effectively, the bubble stores up the economic pain of price adjustments, so it is more disruptive and painful than if we had sorted out the problem of matching price to underlying value as we went along. Instead we mask the need for rebalancing price to value with inflation.

Because humans do not want to use constant weights and measures, our economy is prone to things like stagflation, depression, and hyperinflation. Given that we tend to prefer inflation over deflation, our economy tends toward either stagflation or hyperinflation. But it is important that you understand that both are a direct result of the choices we make. They are not inevitable. Stagflation is a situation where the economy grows slowly without creating enough jobs to employ the work force while at the same time inflation sets in (think

America 1970's). This creates a lot of pain for a lot of people. But it is nothing compared to hyperinflation (think Venezuela 2019).

Since the government can create money (because it is no longer attached to gold), there is always the danger that it will create far more money than is needed. When it does, inflation and eventually hyperinflation set in. But remember that hyperinflation does not start instantly. What starts immediately is the narcotic effect of seeing everything apparently gaining value at a reasonable rate. Unfortunately, we have been trained to think of two or three percent inflation as reasonable. We expect the government to create more money than required by the underlying value of the economy. So, when the government takes extraordinary measures to prevent deflation by injecting extremely large amounts of dollars into the economy as they have done, we do not get upset. But excessive money creation directly undermines the value of our dollars. If the government persists in this, eventually the market decides the government is weakening the value of the dollar too fast for it to be considered a stable measure. When this happens, we have an economic crisis. At that point, it is much more painful and difficult to correct the dollar-value imbalance.

Our leaders in Washington have put us in the position of holding the tiger by the tail. How do you let go of increasing the money supply beyond the actual growth in value of the economy? If we let go of the tiger's tail of over-increasing the money supply, deflation almost inevitably must set in to correct the skewed value of the dollar. No politician wants to bring in the pain of deflation, especially severe deflation. Our human nature almost guarantees that we will hold onto the tiger's tail until it is too late to have anything but a disastrous outcome. The result will be a sudden economic crisis. At that point if the elite running our country fail to fix the value problem (if it's even possible), the crisis becomes a catastrophe. The catastrophe can be anything from depression (money stops flowing) to hyperinflation (money becomes worthless) or some unpredictable combination.

Recall that I said our preference is always toward inflation rather than deflation. It is quite possible we will see hyperinflation before the economists and politicians react to prevent it. We know what causes inflation and how to stop it, nevertheless, many countries have experienced hyperinflation. That is because fundamentally hyperinflation is a political issue, not an economic one. Americans must answer this question: will we as a nation require our political leaders to make the right choices or let them keep covering over the real problems by creating more and more money? So far, excessive money creation is the name of the game. That's why we have such a huge and growing debt burden. Government borrowing creates dollars that flow into the economy making things look prosperous while hiding the underlying destruction of the dollar's value.

If the dollar loses value too quickly, we can easily have hyperinflation. What do you think it will do to our commerce based on trust? Why would I, as a merchant, want your dollars when I know that they will lose half their value before the day is done? I went to Angola once and was there eight days. During that time the local currency lost 50% of its value. I had a hotel bill stated in billions in the local currency, the kwanza! But in fact, the bill was paid in Portuguese escudos. No one wanted the local currency, certainly not the hotel! That's what can happen to the dollar. How can our economy function when we can't use dollars? It can't. It will collapse. In response, our government needs to prevent serious deflation, but injecting more money into the economy just feeds hyperinflation. Venezuela is a good example of what happens. Their GDP decreased 50% in 2015 while inflation climbed so high, it became difficult to measure accurately. As I write this (2019), these trends have continued to the point where Venezuela has in many respects become a failed state. That's what happens when value is ignored.

As a direct result of our fiscal and monetary problems, our currency is on track to lose its status as the world's reserve currency and this will further aggravate our economic problems. As an example, today oil is sold in dollars. We are the only country in the world that has the option to simply create more dollars to buy oil without any regard to any underlying value. In fact, we can simply create dollars out of nothing and that is what we have been doing in the past to pay for our oil.

Thankfully we have essentially become energy independent. But this does not completely shield us from the global market. Other countries import oil priced in dollars. What will happen if the dollar is no longer accepted in international trade? We will no longer have the option to create worthless dollars to make purchases and will then feel the full effect of the true value of the dollar. We will no longer be able to hide its declining value. The increasing price of goods will reflect this true decline. Think inflation.

Unfortunately, America has been systematically destroying the value of its currency for generations, but especially since the 1970s. As we have turned aside from doing honest business based on real value, we have fostered an acceleration in the destruction of the dollar's value. We have congratulated ourselves on our increasing prosperity that turned out to be an illusion. We have seen the technology bubble collapse in the '90s, the housing bubble burst this past decade, and the collapse of the financial bubble more recently. All these were accompanied by severe pain. These have all been warning signs of the danger of doing business based on differing measures. The ultimate judgment on our system will come shortly as our political and intellectual class refuses to be serious about the magnitude of the problems we have created. The remaining 4% of value in the dollar will be destroyed and our economic system will no longer function.

In the next chapter I will describe what could happen and the effects it would have on us personally. Nobody can predict with any certainty what will trigger the catastrophe. Nor can we predict the specific outline of events. We could start with a depression and transition to hyperinflation as the government tries to control the situation by creating more and more dollars. Or we could start with hyperinflation and enter a depression as the government puts the brakes on the economy through interest rate hikes. Maybe we don't have a combination, but instead, have one or the other until equilibrium is restored.

It's clear that without a change in our thinking and actions, an economic crisis will happen. The next chapter is not a prediction of the actual events that will happen. Instead, it is a description of one possible scenario. It helps us to see what kind of effects we can expect to experience. Whatever happens will not be pretty and many people will suffer tremendously. We have been making decisions that defy reality, but reality will not be denied forever. You have been warned.

America Judged

This Monday morning started like many another Monday morning: clear skies, comfortable temperatures during the day, and cool, delightful evening temperatures. This was the kind of Monday weather we all want for every weekend. But this Monday was different. The past week saw inflation running at a 12% annual rate, a rate nearly equal to 1980's painfully high rate. This Monday OPEC announced that oil would no longer be sold in terms of dollars. Overnight the demand for dollars dropped precipitously as other nations no longer needed to buy our dollars to purchase their oil. The dollar immediately lost value against other currencies and the decline in the value continued throughout the week.

America was now forced to buy its imports based on a basket of foreign currencies. But we had to purchase these foreign currencies with a dollar quickly losing value. Within the week, import prices increased 10% in real cost with no end in sight to its rise. The following weeks saw import prices rise another 15%. Oil prices tracked this rise since they were no longer priced in dollars. The American economy quickly started showing worsening signs of higher inflation as the increased cost of imports and oil worked its way through the economy. Americans responded by spending less because more and more of their disposable income went to buying gas for their cars. Retail sales slowed dramatically, and the restaurant industry was hard hit. The recreation industry and tourist destinations experienced a depression as families were forced to cut back on discretionary spending. It looked like the American economy might be headed for serious deflation. The Federal Reserve countered by keeping interest rates at effectively zero and rapidly pumping more dollars into the economy.

The economy struggled along under the pressure of the declining value of the dollar and too much inflation and then— then the *coup de grâce* happened. The leading economies of the world announced that the dollar would no longer be used as the world's reserve currency and would be replaced by special drawing rights. Dollars were no longer needed to buy things like wheat, corn, copper, and a whole host of other products. Overnight the demand for US dollars collapsed completely as other nations no longer needed to hold reserves in dollars in order to transact business. They immediately started dumping these unneeded dollars. We all know what happens when there is too much supply and not much demand. The value drops! The US dollar, which had been losing value from the oil shock, now collapsed completely. It became essentially worthless on the open market, effectively barring the US from functioning in the global marketplace. This disruption quickly spread to the domestic market as even domestic trust in the dollar completely disappeared. Hyperinflation set in as huge amounts of dollars chased fewer and fewer goods and services. What does this mean for you? Let's imagine a plausible scenario.

A few weeks go by and inflation has claimed all your cash, which you used just to buy essentials like food and gasoline for your car. Now what? Reluctantly, you cash in your CDs and money market accounts. After all, who can live without buying food? This buys you a short-term reprieve but simply postpones the inevitable day when you run out of money to pay the ever-increasing prices for essentials. Bread that sold for $2.00 is now up to $20.00 and climbing fast. It doesn't take long for your infusion of cash to disappear with prices like that. You remember fondly filling up your car for only fifty dollars. Now you can't begin to afford the eight hundred dollars it costs. But you know it will cost even more tomorrow.

So far, you are one of the lucky people to still have a job. Payday is here and your paycheck is deposited electronically into your checking account. You have been checking every fifteen or twenty minutes to see when it arrives. You can't afford to leave the money sitting in your account for even a day. Finally, it arrives! Immediately you leave work in order to put gas in your car and buy as much food as you can. Both will be significantly more expensive tomorrow and even tonight when you get off work. Unfortunately, your paycheck is falling farther and farther behind as inflation accelerates. Today, you find your paycheck won't buy enough food to feed you and your family and leave enough money to buy gasoline to get to and from work before the next paycheck. Now what?

Reluctantly, you decide to sell all your blue-chip stocks; things like IBM and Johnson & Johnson that are doing much better than most companies and are not in danger of going out of business. Surely, this will give you enough money to tide you through until the government gets control of the inflation. Of course, nearly everyone else is in the same position as you and they also are forced to sell their stock too. Lots of sellers and very few buyers equal collapsing stock prices. IBM is now selling for a few dollars per share and the price is still trending down. The large infusion of cash you were expecting turns out to be a little infusion of cash that all too quickly gets used up buying essentials. Now what?

You can no longer afford to buy gas for your car, so it is the next thing to go. You sell your two-year-old car for $700 even though before hyperinflation, it would have been worth $20,000. You buy a bike and try getting to work that way, but your company is not doing well and starts laying people off, including you. The $700 you got for your car lasts only a week and no more paychecks are coming. Now what?

The only thing left to sell is your house. It once was worth $350,000 but not today. Other people are selling their houses too. The market is flooded with houses for sale and who has enough money to buy? Lots of sellers and very few buyers equal collapsing housing prices. Someone offers you $25,000 cash so you take it. You move yourself and family into your parent's house. Thank goodness they have already paid off their mortgage. If you can only find some way to feed your family, things might work out all right. Unfortunately, the yard isn't very big, but what yard there is gets turned into a garden to produce fruit and vegetables to help feed the family. But it is not enough by itself. Now what?

Now it is an issue of basic survival, especially in the cities. Riots break out as people start storming grocery stores to steal all the food. Your family is starving so you join in hoping to get anything to eat. Chaos soon spreads and cities become battlegrounds. As chaos reigns, people start coming out of the cities to forage in the countryside. Cows, pigs, horses, dogs, and any edible animal become fair game. Farmers and ranchers close to cities are hard hit and soon are stripped bare. You quickly learn what it means to beg, borrow, or steal in order to survive. Now what?

Today, the news reports the number of murders and suicides hits an all-time high. Word gets out that the family down the street committed murder/suicide as the father put the family out of their misery because he lost hope of being able to survive and couldn't stand to see his family starve to death. Reports are common of older people starving to death in the cities, so you are not totally surprised to hear this news. You even thought of doing the same yourself. Now what?

Finally, the government decides it must put the dollar back on the gold standard so it can stop hyperinflation. New dollars are printed and are set equal to $10,000/ounce of gold. This price is fixed and is not changed. This stabilizes the new dollar, kills inflation, and allows the economy to recover. The result: Americans are much poorer, the economy has contracted 60%, and the country is weaker and no longer a superpower. It is a long and painful process for the economy to recover. The Great Depression looks good compared to what the nation has just experienced.

I, for one, do not know what the coming judgment will actually look like. Complex systems have a way of surprising us. I do know we have more and more ignored reality and the pain it sometimes brings by hiding it from view. But reality just stores up the pain like a fault building to an earthquake. The longer we postpone the pain of adjustment, the worse the earthquake when it comes. Consider yourself warned.

Pt III: Virtue

Better Future

One of the striking things about American society in the twenty-first century is the lack of discussion about virtue. In an age that believes truth is relative, there is no place for virtue or moral excellence. It should be obvious that there can be no moral excellence, no virtue where there is no absolute truth. If everyone can decide on his own truth, then there is no right, no wrong, no good, no bad, just individual choices. This can only lead to chaos, and society can't exist in chaos. There must be at least some order.

As we saw in the previous chapters, the order we have created for ourselves makes us very vulnerable to a financial catastrophe. But it would be strange indeed if ignoring virtue was only a problem for our financial institutions and economy. In fact, ignoring virtue has created a very fundamental problem for Americans. It has blinded us to how we have corrupted our thinking. It has allowed us to employ magical thinking. Magical thinking simply refuses to look at or accept reality, but over time reality always prevails!

The following chapters will look at additional ways magical thinking has influenced us and driven our national debate. It is imperative we understand and root out our magical thinking. It can't bring about the kind of order society needs to be healthy and function properly. Since magical thinking ignores reality, it can cause more than the financial pain previously outlined. Ultimately, it can cause us to lose our freedom, even our country.

It is true there is a great deal of debate and lots of tension on what order America should adopt for itself. It's safe to say our society makes choices, but that doesn't mean society has chosen wisely. The central question we need to ask is what have we chosen to guide us? Since there isn't much talk about virtue or moral excellence, it's difficult to see how we could make wise choices. It is much more likely we have made suboptimal choices. And using magical thinking makes this even more likely.

You might be tempted to say my choices for virtue are just that, my choices. True, but we don't get to choose how the universe works and we don't get to choose to define human nature any way we want. I assure you, when I jump off the roof of my house, I don't fly no matter how hard I try. And if you think human nature has changed significantly in the last two or three thousand years, then you are ignorant of history. Reality doesn't bend to suit such foolishness.

Our magical thinking can't solve the problems we face today. The problems are difficult enough to solve without compounding them with magical thinking. As a nation, we desperately need a discussion about virtue but without neglecting reality. It's the only way to preserve the freedom we have enjoyed since 1776.

In the following chapters we'll discuss some of the issues in America to try to bring clarity to our situation. Clarity about reality and virtue in our thoughts and actions are the way to prevent chaos from engulfing us.

Child, Youth, Adult

Look at the title of this chapter once more and answer a simple question. What does a child have to do in order to become an adult?

I hope you answered, "He or she just has to get older." That is exactly true. It just takes time. The child and youth don't have to do anything to become adults. In fact, there isn't anything they can do to speed up the process. There is no action needed, no choice to be made.

We know that an adult has more rights and more freedom than a child. Is this all we need to know? Do we just say an adult is a person old enough to have full freedom and full rights? Perhaps, but maybe we should examine more closely what we mean by adult.

As I look back on my life in my twenties, I can see I was an adult, but not particularly mature. Yet, there were and are some teenagers and young adults that just seem to have it together, to be more mature. You may have met one or two on your journey through life. I suspect you've probably also come across some people that you wonder when they plan to grow up. (That might have been me in my twenties.) But both the mature and immature are considered adult because of their age.

This hints at a problem that has gotten much worse in America today. A little thought should convince you we think someone is immature because they don't really understand reality. They make poor decisions and suffer the consequences. Too often they don't understand why they had bad consequences. Why are there bad consequences? The simple answer is that reality doesn't bend to their desires. Hopefully they learn from the experience reality gives them and become more mature over time. They learn to adapt their behavior to fit reality. That's maturity.

Let's go beyond our simple answer and look at the dynamics of the situation. Every one of us has emotions, some weak and some strong. Every one of us has a brain capable of intellectual thought that allows us to understand, at least to some degree, the reality around us. And every one of us has a will that propels us forward in life. Better understanding requires we learn more about how the mind, will, and emotions interact as we live our daily lives.

Typically, the immature person is influenced by his emotions. Rather than think through the situation to its logical conclusion, the immature person acts on his desires. The results vary from okay to sometimes catastrophic because emotions are primarily focused on present circumstances without looking too far into the future. Fortunately, reality has a way of forcing us to curb our emotions and let our intellect guide us through the shoals of life. This is how we become more mature.

Let me share with you a little secret. I am very glad I'm wiser than I was in my twenties. Looking back, I sometimes think I got more than my share of difficulties and hard knocks to make me more mature. It's not always wise to be hardheaded!

My sense is that the tension between emotions and intellect is not something new. Rather it seems to be a part of human nature. Our intelligence is something very new in earth's history. It allows us to envision the future in multiple ways, drop the least favorable outcomes, and select from the more favorable outcomes. This ability appears to be uniquely human. It allows us to do a kind of Darwinian evolution in our minds rather than for real, which is much safer for us. And the results are much better, but it requires us to think.

A good sign of maturity is when the intellect overrules the emotions to do what is right or necessary (think virtue or moral excellence). The mind can determine that making a sacrifice now can lead to a much bigger reward later. A sign of childishness is letting emotions rule your actions. A child wants the world to revolve around his desires and wants. A mature person realizes the world can't revolve around him. Because this latter view conforms to reality, a mature person is generally more content and happier. It's the immature person that experiences more friction with the world and is disgruntled and unhappy.

So far, we haven't said much about the will. We assumed the will would be applied to doing mature or immature actions. The implication is the will was guided by either our emotions or our intellect. But there is a third alternative.

This third alternative has grown in my lifetime and is now quite pronounced. What is this alternative? It is letting your will have primary importance. Both emotions and intellect serve what the will wants. The natural outcome of this is that facts are not considered persuasive or even necessary. They are easily dismissed. Worse, the intellect gets used to justify what the will wants, even if it contradicts reality. That's magical thinking.

When the preeminent will is frustrated, the emotions are tied to it in a childish fashion. Indeed, some of what we see today is the adult version of a child's temper tantrum. There is nothing pretty about either and both are ultimately destructive to the individual. Of course, this result is worse for the adult because the adult has a much greater impact on society. When many adults start acting this way, society quickly develops severe problems. Such a group inevitably tries to get reality to change in unrealistic ways rather than adapt to it, which is exactly opposite what a mature person does.

A good example of what I am describing is the current controversy over sex versus gender. Assuming normal chromosomes, there is only male and female, just two sexes. In the past we recognized that children and adolescents sometimes struggle with their identity as male or female. We recognized this as part of a bigger struggle to identify themselves as particular individuals and ultimately as adults. One expected result of this process is becoming comfortable as male or female as we mature into adults. Here we are emphatically not talking about fitting into stereotypes. We are talking about fitting into reality, which is far richer and more complex than simple stereotypes.

Think about what must happen if will is put in charge and intellect and emotions serve it. The natural struggle with identity gets perverted. Now instead of the individual adapting to reality, reality must adapt to the individual's will. It's no longer sex that is the determining factor. It's gender, which is a choice the individual gets to make.

As you would expect, intellect is not allowed to interfere. Thus, there is no thought to looking at the consequences of sex change operations, which results in higher suicide rates. This is treated as irrelevant. It only interferes with the will's desire to bend reality to fit. There can't be any honest debate in society about sex and gender because fundamentally it is an irrational debate.

Magical thinking disconnected from reality guarantees that there is no limiting principle for gender advocates. The rational mind is not allowed to overrule the will. Unintended consequences are ignored. Poor outcomes are irrelevant. Statistics are overlooked. Facts simply don't matter. Reality must bend to their will. This is truly irrational.

I am certainly willing to say that we can change reality. The freedom we enjoy in America today is an historical anomaly. Most people throughout history have lived under authoritarian rule. This is true even today. America's Founding Fathers did change reality and we are the beneficiaries. But the Founding Fathers did not accomplish this as a primary act of will. It was foremost an act of intelligence. These men thought long and hard about human nature and the problems it causes. There was much debate. The result was a rational way to go forward. Only then was it appropriate to use their will to bring about the desired changes. That's not what's happening in America today.

Today in America there is a concerted effort to make man's will preeminent. Often the phrase used is "freedom of choice." But this is a slippery phrase. Sure, I want freedom of choice but in reality, I can't have unlimited freedom. There are some things I can't be allowed to choose. Saying, "Fire!" in a crowded theater is such an example. Making the will preeminent just creates insoluble problems for America. We will discuss some of these as we continue in later chapters.

I remind you, in the first two sections of this book I showed how America has set itself on a course that ultimately leads to financial disaster. But this is really a subset of a much bigger problem we face. Any society that goes about trying to ignore reality or change it irrationally cannot survive. America as a society enjoying its freedom has no guarantee it will continue indefinitely. In fact, history suggests otherwise.

My sense is that we can't solve our financial problems in isolation. We have a problem of the will that needs to be solved. Fundamentally, America needs to stop fighting reality by using magical thinking. That's a battle America can't win. And we can't do that if will is given priority. Instead, we need to act as mature adults.

If virtue or moral excellence is doing what is right, then irrational fighting against reality is not virtuous. It is the very opposite. It can only lead to moral degradation, which is what we see more of in America as time goes by. A good example of this can be seen in the ongoing debate about equality. That's the subject of our next chapter.

Equality or Virtue

We hold these truths to be self-evident, that all men are created equal, that they are endowed by their Creator with certain unalienable Rights, that among these are Life, Liberty and the pursuit of Happiness. — That to secure these rights, Governments are instituted among Men, deriving their just powers from the consent of the governed.

That's the start of paragraph two of the Declaration of Independence adopted by the Congress on July 4, 1776. These are the foundational principles upon which the United States of America was built. But please notice these principles were said to be self-evident. There was no need to justify them or explain them in detail. In fact, only some of these unalienable rights are specifically stated, which means there are others not stated.

For most of US history, these assumptions were accepted. They represented the foundational principles upon which the US Constitution was based. But today, we find the legitimacy of the Constitution itself is questioned. Many of our leaders point out there are apparent contradictions within the Constitution. If there is equality of all men (and women), then how can the Constitution say black slaves are only worth three fifths of their white owners? Doesn't this prove the Constitution is a flawed document that is dated and needs to be rewritten? It certainly shows the power the Southern slave owners had to influence the drafting of the Constitution.

An obvious way to reach any kind of understanding about this is to go back to the foundation and look at the single proposition in the Declaration of Independence: all men are created equal. That's the proposition that is used today to show the Constitution is broken and needs fixing. And it's foundational to many of the conflicts and disagreements we see in our politics, social media, and society at large today.

Both sides of the debate in our country seem to accept this proposition as true, and then argue about how to implement equality. For example, it does seem reasonable and fair to assume that two people doing the same work should be paid the same. And since it's the same work, both should have the same outcome. The outcome, getting paid, becomes an easy way to measure if there is equality. The reality is not that simple. Look at your own experience to understand what I mean. You have probably gone to the same restaurant many times and had different waiters. They were doing the same job. Do you think they all did the job equally well or were some better than others? The reality is that people are not interchangeable cogs in a machine. Equality in job performance is an illusion. It doesn't happen normally.

The use of outcome between two individuals as an indicator of equality naturally leads us to apply the same logic to groups. We conclude there is equality between groups when there are equal outcomes. If the outcomes are not equal, we are forced to assume there is some sort of inequality problem that needs correction. But just as individuals are not identical, neither are groups. Individuals are not a cog in a machine, and neither are groups. If you watch any team sports, you can see this truth. The teams (groups of people) are not identical. Some are better, some are worse. If they were all the same, we probably wouldn't bother watching.

Unfortunately, the argument for equal outcomes has gained considerable acceptance in America despite its obvious flaws. More and more our government, our courts, and public opinion have accepted the idea that outcomes should be equal. When outcomes aren't, this is considered proof there is discrimination. But this is really an example of setting our will over our intellect. It ignores reality. Let me explain.

There is a fundamental problem with assuming equality must mean equal outcomes. Despite the Declaration of Independence, we are not entitled to assume all men are created equal. We've already given two examples of the inherent inequality of people (waiters, sports teams). Look around and see for yourself if all men are created equal. It's obviously not true. We are not all gifted athletes or brilliant as Einstein. We are not all tall, or thin, or bald. Take a minute and name some other characteristics that vary. We are not all equal and we live in societies that are not equal either. Just look at Venezuela today (2019). It was the richest nation in South America. Now it's the poorest as it nears total collapse. Societies are not and cannot all be equal. Do you need more proof?

The industrial revolution didn't start in Western countries by accident. Western culture developed what became known as the scientific method because the early scientists wanted to understand God's creation. The Bible commanded them to take control of the world, but it also required them to be good stewards. This propelled them to seek understanding. Other societies before them had other priorities and this is still true to this day.

A case in point is the story of Chinese Admiral Zheng He who led seven naval expeditions between 1405 and 1433. His first expedition left port on July 11, 1405. This was no small undertaking. The fleet consisted of 317 ships and 27,800 men. The largest ships apparently were about 400 feet long. Imagine if you can, treasure ships, horse ships, supply ships, troop transports, warships, patrol boats, and water tankers. When this fleet showed up, it made an impression! These expeditions went as far as East Africa (and possibly sent a few ships to West Africa) and extended Chinese influence over a wide area. China could have extended its influence even farther in distance and longer in time.

It all ended under Xuande Emperor (~1426-1435 AD). The last major expedition occurred under his rule in 1431. On the return voyage from this trip, Admiral He died (~1433). Since Xuande Emperor had concluded the voyages contradicted the established rules of the dynasty, he had ordered them stopped and the ships burned. Thus, there was no need to chronicle the exploits of the ships or Zheng He. And the story of Admiral He faded into obscurity for several centuries.

It should be obvious that China chose a much different path than the western nations chose just a few years later. We can argue about which was better, or successful, or least harmful, or do so in numerous other ways. These don't matter for my conclusion. Societies are not all equal for the simple reason that they are each unique. They have different values and seek different goals. China chose a different destiny than Spain,

Portugal, England, etc. China was not discriminated against in this. Thus, it makes no sense to say nations or their peoples should have equal outcomes. Societies don't strive for equal outcomes because they value and want different things

Perhaps a practical analogy can help you see my point. When I was growing up in West Hartford, Connecticut, our backyard had a pear tree, one red apple tree, and two green apple trees. Don't you think it would be odd to say we had a severe problem with our trees because the outcomes were so different? We expect the pear tree to produce pears and the apple trees to produce apples. The goal of the pear tree is to produce pears, not apples. In the same way China chose different goals than the western European nations, and the results were not equal. This is what we should expect of groups rather than complain about unequal outcomes. The same thing applies to individuals. They don't all strive for the same goal or want the same things.

What does all of this say about, "We hold these truths to be self-evident, that all men are created equal"? Can it be true all men are created equal? No! When the writers of the Declaration of Independence wrote this, they could not mean, nor did they believe, this was literally true. They understood people had different levels of skill, different levels of intelligence, different levels of strength. They were not stating a general principle that was literally true. Their argument was that men (and women) are equal before God because God gave them unalienable rights. This idea leads naturally to the idea that laws are derived from the authority of the governed. This implies all are equal before the law or should be in a fair, just society. But it does not mean the outcomes should be the same.

I hope you can see that we can't replace equality of outcomes with equality of opportunity because they are both flawed. A little thought should convince you of that. We don't let children have equal opportunity for driving or voting because they are not ready to handle such responsibility. Can you see the inherent problem with equal opportunity? We can't have equality of opportunity because people are not all equal. Children are not equal to adults. And not all adults are equal either. We can't let adult alcoholics drive cars whenever they want. Nor can we have a society based on equality of opportunity or outcome because people are fundamentally unequal. Nature shows us the norm is inequality, not equality. We go against nature when we try to impose equality indiscriminately. This can only be done at the expense of freedom. But more and more that is what we have been doing in the US. We have ignored reality. We have set our will over our intellect and essentially become irrational. We demand an equality that can never be.

The principle of equality seems to represent one of the serious internal controversies we have here in the United States. Lots of time and energy have been spent arguing for or against one side or the other. And neither side questions if equality is the most important issue. It's just assumed that this is the proper argument to have. And it is one of the reasons America is in danger of being judged.

The truth is equality is not foundational and our arguments over it neglects the real discussion we need to have. But this is not the same thing as saying equality is unimportant. It is important, but it's not foundational despite what the Declaration of Independence says. I say this because nobody really believes in equality!

I can hear you now saying, "That's not true. Of course, I believe in equality." Do you really? Do you want the ten-year-old boy down the street driving a car? Or the twelve-year-old girl voting on election day? Maybe you think I'm being unfair because I've mentioned children, although they are people too. Let's try a few more questions. Do you want everyone in the United States on election day eligible to vote or just US citizens? What about a paranoid schizophrenic living under a bridge? He can't understand the ballot. Do you think he should vote? Or what about the Alzheimer patient who doesn't even know what country he lives in?

I flew to another country recently and had to go through a security checkpoint to get to my plane. Maybe you think everybody should be allowed to fly too? Do you want the terrorist trying to board your plane to have the same opportunity as you? I'm sorry. I don't want the terrorist to have that same opportunity to get on the plane! Do you want him to have the same outcome as me? What relevance does equality have in this or any of the previous cases? Equality of outcomes makes no sense and equality of opportunity seems inappropriate in many cases.

We may say we believe all men are created equal. But what we really mean is all men are created equal within reasonable restrictions. And that is what we are really arguing about or should be. What are the reasonable restrictions? How do we derive them? How do we justify them? How do we apply them consistently and fairly? And all the while we pretend equality is foundational when we know it is not. It is always restricted in some way.

The fact that equality has restrictions should not really surprise us. Our lives require us to practice balance between competing interests. I love to vacation, but I must balance this against the need to make money. I love to eat desert, but I must balance this against becoming too obese. I find maintaining that particular balance seems to be a struggle, especially the older I get!

It is imperative that we recognize there are competing interests and life requires balance. Our preoccupation with equality prevents us from thinking about and accepting balance. But any discussion of balance inevitably leads to a discussion about how we are going to determine proper balance. And the only way to do that is to talk about virtue because there can't be balance without virtue. Do you understand? Since we need to do what is right, we must have a discussion on the meaning of virtue before we can ever decide what equality really means.

Virtue or moral excellence could generate a lot of discussion by itself without talking about the need for balance or the problem of equality. But let's not get bogged down in endless controversy. Let's agree for now that virtue means following the Golden Rule: do unto others as you want them to do unto you. It is a rule found in many religions of the world, which means many people in many places and different times agree this is a good definition of virtue.

Did you notice that the Golden rule says nothing about equality of any kind? And it only implies balance as an outcome of applying the rule consistently. But think about how this could change the conversation in the U.S. today. Think of how it would change the way people act towards each other. It certainly would remake our political discussions and eliminate some of the tension. And it certainly would quell the rising political violence. Your fellow citizen is not your enemy.

As we have set our will above our intellect, we have indeed become more irrational. We set about using our minds to find ways to impose our will without regard to any facts, especially contrary facts. This inevitably leads to ideas that seem right but are actually detrimental to our wellbeing. Let me give you one extreme example.

In recent years we have seen a very bad idea take hold in people's minds. It is an idea that left unchecked will destroy America. That's because it is the opposite of the Golden Rule. It is the idea that hate speech should be disallowed because it is not really protected speech under the First Amendment to the Constitution. Of course, the reality is that the First Amendment was specifically designed to prevent speech from being disallowed by government and those in authority. In other words, it was designed to protect "hate speech." Why? Because no one person or group of people is able to define "hate speech" in a way that everyone can accept. You may say things that others say is hateful. Do you want them telling you your talk is not allowed?

It is the Golden Rule that should guide us. It tells us that we need to let other people talk even when we strongly disagree with them. It is virtue that gives us the balance we need to live in a free society. And it is virtue that checks our desire to put our will over our thinking.

Our focus on equality has warped our thinking and lets us forget virtue. But this has led us away from reality into fantasy. There can be no real balance in fantasy and that's what we see in America today, a lack of balance. We need to take to heart that no nation can survive if its goal is fantasy!

Hierarchy

Foundations of Hierarchy

In the last chapter we saw how our desire to have equality of outcomes has led us to will this to be so. But our thinking shows us clearly that this is an unrealistic goal. It defies reality. This is not the only example of applying our wills to an unrealistic goal. Another example is the trendy idea of patriarchy.

Patriarchy has been redefined to mean the oppression of women, minorities, etc. by men, particularly white men. It is portrayed as a naked application of power. With this as a starting point and foundation, it makes sense to look for examples of oppression in our society and correct the situation. Not so surprising, one way this is done is by looking at equality of outcomes! We've already seen how this leads us astray. It should not surprise us then if the idea of patriarchy itself leads us astray.

A mature person thinks about patriarchy from a commonsense perspective. Such a person uses his/her will only after using their mind to develop an understanding of the facts. This means understanding hierarchy of which patriarchy is just one example. Let's follow this thread and develop our understanding.

You've probably heard the term alpha male. This comes directly from the hierarchy found in dogs, wolves and other animals. Heck, even chickens have a pecking order! In nature the hierarchy is founded on power. The alpha male is number one by virtue of strength and the ability to dominate others. Patriarchy as defined above fits this mold quite naturally.

People set on using their will instead of reason stop thinking about hierarchy at this point and use it to justify opposing patriarchy. The mature person uses their mind to continue to understand hierarchy better. Some thought should convince you that hierarchy does not have to be based on power. It can also be based on competence. Let me give you an example.

I spent many years playing the trombone and became very proficient at it. In high school I played in the All-State High School Orchestra. This was quite an achievement reserved for the three best high school trombonists in Connecticut. As an adult, I have enjoyed going to hear the Houston Symphony many times. At the beginning of each concert, the concert master comes out with his or her violin, takes a bow, and then tunes the orchestra. The concert master is the principle or best violinist. I assure you this person wasn't appointed to this chair because of their strength and ability to dominate others. The concert master earns the principle violin seat by competence. Indeed, the Houston Symphony is made up of musicians who all earned their positions by the competence they displayed with their chosen instrument. They all had musical ability and worked hard to develop it to a fine level. They are very competent musicians and have joined a hierarchy based on competence.

Let's not get lazy and end our search for understanding hierarchy just yet. There's more to learn. As I think about my experience working for a large oil company, I recognize the obvious hierarchy. There was a CEO, senior managers, mid-level managers, line managers, and workers. In general, a person needed to be reasonably competent in order to rise through the ranks. But they also had to be good at exercising power and not be intimidated by others. This is interesting because it suggests hierarchy can be based on a hybrid of power and competence. Both are required to advance in a large company.

I want to remind you that the person who has allowed his/her will to be primary doesn't let the mind think through problems properly. Yes, it's true patriarchy could be a hierarchy based solely on power as claimed. But there are two other possibilities that need to be examined. Patriarchy could be based on one of these. We will have more to say on this in the next chapter.

Understanding Hierarchy

There are many problems inherent in a hierarchy of power, at least as far as humans are concerned. This is not the place to do an exhaustive analysis. Nevertheless, looking at some of the reasons is very revealing. Power hierarchies consolidate power and decision making towards the top of the hierarchy far from many of the problems. And often the decisions that come down don't fit the problems particularly well. This disconnect is made worse when the authorities simply ignore or fail to see problems. The result is a large segment of society becoming disillusioned with the hierarchy.

The real Achilles heel of human power hierarchies is their disconnect from competence. People are not promoted for competence, but because of their ability to use power. It's not hard to see that after some time those excluded from power have more competent people than the elites exercising power. This is an explosive situation: a disillusioned majority that has a larger number of competent people compared to those in charge. When the disillusioned finally revolt against the minority in the upper hierarchy, the results are often a catastrophic collapse of the power hierarchy. Examples of this are the collapse of East Germany and the Soviet Union. Power hierarchies are inherently brittle rather than flexible and robust.

The obvious antidote to forming a brittle power hierarchy is to let the competent people rise into the upper hierarchy. America has traditionally had a hierarchy that generally included competence. It has proved to be markedly resilient and stable, having even survived the Civil War. If America shows anything, it's that hierarchies must include competence as a defining characteristic for long term stability.

Unfortunately, today in America we see a whole segment of society defining politics as a power game. The application of force is justified by the desirable end of gaining power to effect desirable outcomes. The supposedly good end always justifies whatever means are used to get there. It is simply might makes right. Such people are not prone to listen to others in humility. If they did, they could learn useful and interesting things. The truth is these people believe in and want a power hierarchy and don't recognize the peril it brings. They see themselves as power brokers in this power hierarchy.

There is one more flaw we need to look at in power hierarchies. Power by its very nature does not like to be constrained. Unconstrained power lets those that exercise power believe they are always right. That's why power needs to be constrained by checks and balances. But there is also an internal constraint that needs to be present: a sense of fair play. More and more in America the sense of fair play is being lost. It is being lost because the people who seek a power hierarchy do not like to be constrained and more and more have abandoned fair play. This also creates an unstable society. The middle ground necessary for debate, discussion, and consensus building shrinks leaving a polarized society. This can easily lead to a soft civil war, which we have already. If the middle ground shrinks too much, then debate and consensus building cannot happen. The only option left is the raw exercise of power. It can look like the Civil War, or it could look like a tyrannical government controlling the people. The raw exercise of power happened once in American and it can happen again.

Just how important is fair play for the stability and success of America or any robust social hierarchy? Try this experiment to find out. Sit two people down and tell them one person will be given $100, which he must share with the other person or they both lose the money. There is no negotiating allowed. The person with the money decides only once how he will share the money. There is no redo. The person receiving the money can only accept the offer or reject it. If the person rejects the offer, they both lose the money. Under these rules you would expect the second person to agree to whatever he is offered because then he would receive free money. You would predict the second person to be happy even just receiving one free dollar. But that's not what happens. The second person rejects all such small offers and essentially refuses to play the game to get richer. When asked why he didn't accept the dollar, the second player says the other person wasn't playing fair! He would rather not play the game at all and let them both lose the money. The little money wasn't enough of a reward, or bribe, to entice the second person to play an inherently unfair game. It wasn't enough that the money was free. Let me emphasize this. The problem was the person with the money "wasn't playing fair."

Do you see what this says about power hierarchies? Power doesn't have to play fair. When it doesn't, it creates a people willing to say they won't play the game anymore. This is a major cause of instability. Power hierarchies over time create a disillusioned populace with competent people that become willing to stop playing by the rules set up by the leaders of society. I think this helps explain why there is a sudden collapse of power hierarchies. First, the majority has a lot of competent people to lead them. Second, they are disillusioned with the power brokers and decision makers. And third, they are prone to say they won't play society's games anymore. When the populace realizes how many people don't want to play by the existing rules, they rise up in rebellion. When this starts, the change can be very rapid indeed. This explains why East Germany collapsed so quickly. It also helps us understand the fall of communism in Eastern Europe and the collapse of the Soviet Union.

As I look at America today, I see a federal bureaucracy that has become less accountable and more powerful. And the number of examples of incompetence has increased along with the number of ill-fitting rules. Thankfully, the latter have been decreasing recently. Still, overall, these are signs of a government that increasingly resembles a power hierarchy. And this trend has been going on for over a century. The signs of instability are growing. What's the solution?

The antidote is certainly not to make the hierarchy even more of a power hierarchy. But this is exactly what many in America want. Take the example of patriarchy. Since this is perceived as a power hierarchy, it must take a bigger power to break it. A segment of American society has arisen and said we will not play by the existing rules of patriarchy. They want a different power hierarchy to effect the needed changes. They want the power of the state exercised through new laws, rules, and education to break the patriarchy. The only problem is that the patriarchy as perceived doesn't exist. They have set their will to make a major social change but refuse to think clearly about hierarchies and about patriarchy in particular, which we discuss in the next chapter.

As we leave this chapter, let's remind ourselves that social hierarchies based solely on power are too brittle to last. They must include competence and fair play to give them the flexibility and support they need to survive long term. We do know that patriarchy in some fashion has been around for a very long time. This shows us patriarchy is not likely to be a power hierarchy as it is portrayed. Let's keep this in mind as we study patriarchy more closely in the next chapter.

Patriarchy

Today in America there is a concerted effort by some to claim society's hierarchy is a social construct made by men for the purpose of oppressing women. Such people even have a name for it: patriarchy. It stands to reason since men created and perpetuate patriarchy, it must have as its root cause a toxic masculinity. Men created the hierarchy of oppression because they had the power to do so. This makes them the problem!

I hope you see that this view of hierarchy requires us to believe patriarchy is a social construct based on the exercise of power. Both are in opposition to important facts mentioned about hierarchy in the last chapter. Regarding the first, either hierarchy is a construct of nature or it is a more recent social construct of toxic masculinity. It can't be both. There is no doubt the facts from nature support hierarchy as far older than mankind. It most definitely is not a recent social construct of powerful men asserting their toxic masculinity to impose a hierarchy, now conveniently called patriarchy. Such efforts to blame men are aimed at the wrong problem.

If we dig more deeply into the ideas of toxic masculinity and patriarchy, we discover a second fundamental flaw. Patriarchy as defined is considered an exercise of power for the express purpose of controlling women and children. The belief is that patriarchy fundamentally rests only on power. Those that have power are high in the hierarchy and those that don't are lower. As we saw, a cursory look at nature suggests that this is true. There really is an alpha dog in a dog pack. But patriarchy's extraordinary longevity suggests it's not a simple power hierarchy.

There is no question that we should strive to make society more just, fair, and compassionate. But we can't possible do this if our basic understanding of fundamental problems is flawed. Yet, that is precisely what we are trying to do in America today. We are making changes to society based on a flawed understanding of reality. And reality will not change to accommodate our flawed thinking. Reality demands that we get our thinking straight or pay the consequences. It's our choice.

I want to give you an example from the patriarchy debate of what I am talking about. But before I do, I need to remind you that this section of the book has shown the imbalance between our mind, will, and emotions. Most of us recognize that letting our emotions control our lives is counterproductive. It leads to an unhappy life. But most of us fail to recognize that letting our will control our lives is also counterproductive in the long run. The reason is that putting either emotions or will in control inevitably leads to irrational decisions. Reality doesn't change to fit our magical thinking and irrational decisions. That's the problem we face with patriarchy today.

The concept of a power-based patriarchy prevalent today is essentially irrational. It is based on letting the will be in control rather than examining the situation, looking at facts, and evaluating outcomes. If the mind is not allowed to affect the will, then our behavior can't remain logical. Instead emotions are used to support what we will to do even when it is irrational. Let me show you a good example of what I mean.

On average women earn 80% of what a man earns. You've probably heard that statistic multiple times. On its face this hardly seems fair and a simple explanation is to blame it on the established patriarchy. This statistic is said to prove that patriarchy is inherently malevolent. It is clear proof of toxic masculinity in action. Men are simply oppressing women because they have power and choose to do so. This evokes our sense of fair play being violated. Framed this way, it's easy to let emotions propel you to say the pay gap isn't fair.

Let's take a step back from our emotions and let's put our will on hold before we start to force changes in our society. We do this to give time for our minds to think through the problem. Let's accept the 80% pay statistic and start looking for its causes. The first thing we notice is blaming pay disparity on patriarchy assigns all the blame to a single cause. This could be true but only if all the other possible causes have been ruled out.

But that is precisely what the advocates of patriarchy have not done. They refuse to consider any other explanation and set about apply their will to solve the perceived problem. How is it possible to arrive at a good, equitable solution when you don't even know the real causes of the 80% pay gap? You can't.

Any social scientist worthy of the name does a multivariate analysis of the pay gap problem. This is just a fancy way to say he looks at multiple possible causes and tries to determine how much of a contribution each makes to the pay disparity. Could patriarchy contribute to the problem? Sure. Is it the only factor determining the outcome? Not likely. What other things may contribute to the result?

Give it some thought and name one other possible explanation for differences in pay between men and women. Did you think about the number of hours worked on average? The reality is men work longer hours on average than women. We should expect them to be compensated for this extra work. That's what equal pay for equal work should demand.

Multi-variant analysis also suggests that the biggest predicters of success (and higher pay) are actually competence and less agreeableness. Since women on average are more agreeable than men, this has a significant impact on their pay. The work place is a competitive environment, which means it's not always good to be agreeable. Sometimes you need to be disagreeable and fight for a better job or more pay. And women can do this if they want.

I hope you see that this opens up the discussion even more. Why is it so necessary to be competitive? Is that desirable or not? Shouldn't we all learn to be more agreeable? Now we're starting to have a real conversation about real problems. Blaming the pay gap on patriarchy just relieves us of the responsibility to think through the problem adequately to understand reality. But that's necessary if we want to have a society that doesn't continually fight with reality. In fact, that's precisely what America is doing with patriarchy: using our will to fight against reality.

It's past time for America to put logical constraints on our will. Discussions on malevolent patriarchy and toxic masculinity lead us into fantasy. In truth, we desperately need to understand reality if we want to succeed as a just and compassionate society.

Patriarchy is just one example of how our magical thinking contradicts reality and clouds our understanding. Another example can be seen in how we think about greed, the subject of the next chapter.

Greed or Self-Interest

As I look back on my teenage years and on into my twenties, I am amazed at my foolishness and lack of understanding. Somehow, I reached adulthood thinking that making lots of money was a sign of greed. Companies proved they were greedy because they often had sales where the normal price was discounted. To me this was proof they could sell their products cheaper but were greedy and wanted to make a bigger profit. And what about the senior management? They must be greedy too because of their very fat salaries while their workers struggled to make ends meet.

Now I'm older and wiser, at least in some circumstances. I now know a company that doesn't make enough money to innovate and evolve dies a slow or not so slow death. A good example of what I am talking about is Sears. For 150 years Sears was a leader in retail sales. Their innovation of using catalog sales led to their rapid growth. Their failure to adapt to the modern equivalent of catalog sales, the online store, has hastened their slow decline.

Karl Marx had it wrong when he called profits excess capital withheld from the workers. Companies go bankrupt without profits. Even non-profit organizations must have profits to stay in business. They are just somewhat limited with what they can and can't do with the profits. If we focus on profits and worry about what is too much profit, we lose necessary perspective. The result is we have a difficult time distinguishing between greed and self-interest.

In our present context greed is an excessive desire for more money. But that's a poor definition because how do you define an excessive desire? All too often, the person complaining defines what they don't like in someone else as being excessive. But that doesn't mean it's truly excessive. And all too often, this simply confuses self-interest with greed.

How are we to avoid such bias? Let's start by looking more closely at self-interest. A simple diagram may help:

My money spent on me	Others' money spent on me
My money spent on others	Others' money spent on others (think government)

When I spend money on things I want, I usually take care to make sure I get exactly what I want. When I buy a present for someone else, I try to get something nice. But if he or she doesn't like it they can take it back and exchange it for something else. I won't work as hard to make sure they get what they want because I don't have the time or energy and it's not really necessary. Yes, I'm concerned about getting value for my money but not nearly as much as when I buy for myself.

Let's take the next step and say I could buy something for myself using someone else's money. Maybe I won the lottery, or a rich uncle died and said his estate would let me buy anything I wanted up to one million dollars. I think I would go out and buy some exotic sports car with the money and I wouldn't worry too much about price! Where's all the care I have when I use my own money to buy a car?

There is still one more box to look at. This shows the case where I can spend someone else's money on other people or other projects without spending any of my money. Let's say I'm given one million dollars to help others. I'm not allowed to keep any of the money for myself. I'm sure I could find suitable charities around town. I doubt I would take the time to make sure it is the best use of the money. After all, it's not my money and I am using it to do good anyway!

I hope you see that I described the four boxes from highest self-interest to lowest self-interest. But if we label self-interest greed, then spending other people's money on other people must be preferred as the least greedy way.

Unfortunately, it is also the least efficient use of the money. And that is exactly the problem we have today.

We teach our children that working for government is better than working for "greedy" capitalists. Yet, our chart shows us government is the least likely to spend our money wisely. People think it makes sense to take money from the people with money and give it to the government to care for the less fortunate. But government is the least likely to spend this money wisely. There's little self-interest in government bureaucracies in doing so. Experience shows us the truth of this. Governments are inherently wasteful. It is far better to let wealthy people spend their money directly on charity. They would do a better job of it.

Do you want proof of this? Consider one recent example: The Veterans Administration. Management at some hospitals were keeping two sets of books. One book was used publicly to show what a good job they were doing – and just coincidentally justifying bonuses for management! The other set of books contained the real list of veterans requesting service. Some veterans were never treated at all and simply died. Wait times to see a doctor were measured in months, not days or weeks. This was a corrupt, inefficient system. Why was this so? The incentives were certainly wrong. The government was using other people's money on others, the veterans. It was bound to become inefficient and wasteful.

Unfortunately, our lack of understanding about greed and self-interest colors our thinking about capitalism. What we have today in America is more and more a form of corrupt capitalism. It's crony capitalism or "rent seeking" capitalism where companies and individuals bypass market capitalism by getting government to spend money or mandate a certain outcome. This distorts the markets by distorting self-interest. It is a way to prevent market capitalism from working correctly.

Market capitalism focuses solely on the process of buying and selling and is totally indifferent to the outcome. Sometimes the outcome seems less than ideal. The problem is that government tries to correct "problems" and in doing so makes it impossible for normal capitalism to correct itself. The reason is quite simple. Economic decisions always involve self-interest. This deserves some serious consideration.

Yesterday I went to my favorite grocery store and bought this week's grocery list. I took care about what I bought because I bought it for me (self-interest)! But I can guarantee that the grocery store didn't sell me the groceries because they like me. They didn't sell me groceries because I'm such a nice person (or not). They didn't sell me groceries because I live in the local neighborhood. They sold me groceries so they could make a profit and stay in business! They followed their own self-interest. That is not greed!

Consider the grocery store that is greedy. What happens? Their prices are slightly higher, or their quality is lower for the same price. In the short run this may work but consumers act in their own self-interest. They will take their business to a store with better prices or quality. The greedy store goes out of business.

There is an obvious conclusion we can draw from this. Good business is always a win-win situation. I got the groceries I needed. The store got the money they need to make a profit and stay in business. Bad business is always a win-lose situation. The greedy grocery store succeeds for a while. They get the money they need to make a profit and then some and I get goods worth less than what I spent. That makes me the loser in the situation.

The beauty of capitalism is that it is naturally self-correcting. At any point in time there are imbalances but over time these get corrected. Shortages get filled, excesses dissipate, and discipline is administered – the greedy store fails! Government only really needs to protect us against fraud. The greedy store is not committing fraud because they think, incorrectly, that they have created a win-win situation. Fraud starts with the intent to create a very one-sided win-lose situation. Fraud is a good example of real greed in action. But companies making lots of money giving us what we want is not greed. It is self-interest on both sides, company and consumer. The result is a win-win situation that benefits both parties.

Our failure to understand the difference between self-interest and greed is causing our society lots of unnecessary stress. We need to understand the only way to change a self-interest, win-win situation is by picking winners and losers. The long-term effect of this is to decrease the economy's growth. It makes us all poorer than we would be if we let people follow their own self-interest and let companies do the same. Please understand, picking winners and losers only happens when we override someone's self-interest and make it a win-lose situation. Let's not confuse the issue by calling self-interest greed. It's not and never will be.

Notice that calling self-interest greed makes it easy to justify applying our will to correct a perceived problem. It also makes it easy to avoid the hard work required for true understanding. What's the result? Today there are many professors at universities and prominent politicians that argue for socialism because of the false notion that capitalism promotes greed and exploitation. They work hard to bring about change based on simplistic thinking that contradicts reality. Self-interest is not greed!

This is yet another example of letting our will rule over our intellect. These people ignore known facts and conjure up a fantasy. But fantasy always conflicts with reality, sometimes in catastrophic ways. Stalin, Mao, and Pol Pot killed millions of their countrymen in pursuit of a socialism fantasy!

America was founded on the idea that people should be allowed to follow their own self-interest, Unfortunately, today we have a whole segment of society pushing to give government more and more control. The predictable result is Americans are becoming less and less free to follow their own self-interest and our economy has become less efficient.

As we become more polarized as a nation, it becomes harder and harder to look for truth objectively. It also becomes more and more difficult to have an honest conversation about greed and self-interest. That's why we need to embrace virtue. Virtue shows us that others are not our enemies. They need to be treated with respect. This is how we make it possible to have a discussion or debate about greed versus self-interest. Without this debate, we can't arrive at a good understanding of reality and won't agree on the proper course of action. That's the real problem we face in America today.

Envy or Results

We have been studying virtue, following the Golden Rule, while looking at some contemporary problems in America. Another such problem is the growing problem of envy. At first glance envy might not seem like it breaks the Golden Rule. I may envy my neighbor with the new Porsche, but that doesn't harm him. And if I had the Porsche and he envied me, that's just fine with me! So, what's the problem?

The problem is envy is an emotional response and emotions motivate us to act. I envy because I want but don't have. My emotions cause me to try to change the situation, and this is where the problems start. There are two ways I can try to change the situation. I can try to change my circumstances so I can afford a new Porsche. And that's hard work! Of course, it would be a good result. Or I can decide my neighbor has some unfair advantage or unusual luck and should share his good fortune. Do you care to guess which way envy motivates us to go? I bet you guessed right. Envy is considered a negative emotion for a reason.

Envy motivates me to penalize my neighbor. Think about it. Don't you agree the rich should pay their fair share? Let's tax them. Or maybe we're more direct in our attack. Maybe we think he got rich by not paying his employees a living wage. We should right this wrong. Let's raise the minimum wage. Unfortunately, our envy betrays us because it has blinded us to reality. But how is this possible?

Earlier we talked about complex systems. We noted that economic systems are non-linear, which is a fancy way of saying the results we get now will affect the results we get in the future. And one of the reasons that happens is because humans are involved. A proper understanding of economics must account for people and their motivations and actions. Envy blinds us to this truth.

Think about this carefully. If we try to penalize our friend with the Porsche, we will change his behavior in ways that we may not be able to predict. And even if we predict his actions correctly, we may still experience unintended consequences. Let's do a hypothetical case to see how this could work out.

This year we decide to tax Porsche man at a 70% tax rate on his income. Our plan is to use the money to increase government child support payments, which I just happen to need so I think this is a good idea. Maybe I'll be able to buy that Porsche after all! This all looks good on paper but doesn't include Porsche man as an active participant, which he is. Let's put him into the equation. Our prediction assumes Porsche man doesn't alter his behavior, but Porsche man decides it's not worth working so hard only to keep 30% of what he earns. He lays off his secretary, closes his business, retires, and his income falls below the 70% tax rate. Our tax windfall disappears because Porsche man decided to make it disappear. We made a bad assumption, which was really a prediction about Porsche man's future behavior. Our envy caused us to back a plan that didn't accomplish its stated goal. Worse, it decreased economic activity guaranteeing less tax revenue now and in the future. Alternatively, maybe this time my envy paid off. With my extra child support, I bought my own Porsche. I did it by making the country poorer. That's not a good long-term strategy.

We just saw the worst-case scenario, but let's be generous to our plan. Let's say that Porsche man continues to work. We pat ourselves on the back thinking our plan worked. But we haven't looked at any unintended consequences. Porsche man was going to expand his business and open a new office in another city. With the tax rate change, he no longer had the money to open the new office. Now multiply this by all the businessmen making such decisions. Within a very short time the lost revenue from the additional businesses not started is much bigger than the amount we receive from the 70% tax rate. We end up worse off, not better off because we let envy guide our thinking.

Our Porsche man scenario still has more to teach us. I supported the 70% tax rate because I envied my neighbor. But I also supported it because it wouldn't affect me. Indeed, even when Porsche man reacted unexpectedly to the tax rate hike, his decisions didn't affect me personally. Another way to say this is I had no skin in the game. I could gain from my envy, but I couldn't lose anything. But how does this match up to the Golden Rule? Would I want someone to take 70% of my income in hopes of getting something out of it? Would I like it if he had no skin in the game and was simply motivated by envy and greed? Virtue tells me envy easily leads to actions that are unvirtuous and even harmful.

Our scenario shows us we don't even need to think about envy to decide our 70% tax plan isn't a good plan. We only need to look at the results. Based on expected total income, we can estimate how much a 70% tax rate should bring in. When the actual number starts coming in, we only need to ask if it falls short significantly. If it does, then we can be sure the plan is not a good one and is most likely hurting rather than helping people. The tax hike should be repealed. But that's hard to do. Why? Because people blinded by envy are not persuaded by facts, even when the facts are right in front of them. They let their will have control over their thinking.

Let's generalize this because it is an important point. Envy makes us blind to reality in several important ways:

1. We support policies that don't cost us anything but offer us potential rewards. We are "gaming the system." Heads, I win; tails, you lose! By its very nature, it is not an equitable situation.
2. We fail to account for the actions of the people who are affected negatively by the changes. And we fail to account for unintended consequences. Our policies pull people down rather than build people up.
3. We ignore the results of our choices. We may feel good about being fair or compassionate or just, but we divorce this from the results.

Negative results should lead to positive change,
but envy won't allow this.

These same considerations can be used to view any of our actions as individuals or the actions we take as a group. Virtue shows us the each of the three problems is caused by breaking the Golden Rule. And that suggests there is a remedy.

Our focus on equality as a culture has caused us to stumble badly. It has allowed us to legitimize envy. But in the process, we routinely break the Golden Rule and often remain unaware of this fact. We focus on equality and almost totally ignore virtue. But it is virtue that can get us to make better decisions individually and corporately as a nation. It is virtue that gets us better results. It is virtue that helps us keep our will from getting ahead of our thinking. And it is virtue that can help us see the pitfalls of envy and greed.

Education

If I ask the question, what is the purpose of education, you will probably say something like it is to broaden our children's experience or to expose them to more things to prepare them better for life. These answers put our focus on experiences that our children and youth can have. We seem determined that our children be given all the opportunities we can provide to ensure their success. We often wonder, are we doing all we can to broaden their experience and prepare them for life in our increasingly complex, and diverse society? That is how we think; that is part of our focus on youth and the youth culture in America. It is, at least in part, one expression of our youth idolatry.

In one sense this simply flies in the face of reality. As we go through childhood and our teen years, we grow in potential. We learn to play sports. We develop hobbies and activities to build skill: music, dance, theater, carpentry, computer programming, etc. All of these increase the potential of what we can do as adults. That seems to be the reason behind our desire to give our children lots of opportunity to try things and develop interests. The inherent problem is that as we finally prepare to become adults, we must make sacrifices and narrow our focus. We can't do all the things that interest us if we want to succeed in life.

Let me give you an example from my own life. After graduating high school, I took scuba diving lessons and bought all the equipment I needed. One year later I got more involved in mountain climbing in a serious way. It claimed my time, money, and effort. I didn't have the time or money to actually do any scuba diving. Eventually my scuba diving equipment was stolen. This experience showed me that life forced me to make decisions to narrow my focus. Sure, I could have taken up scuba diving later. But the truth is family and work became a higher priority. I suppose now I could take up scuba diving instead of writing books, but somehow that seems too frivolous. If I get a chance on vacation, I'll take a day or two excursion for scuba diving.

Life truly has narrowed my opportunities. In order to succeed at life, I've had to make choices. More importantly, I've had to make choices that required sacrifice. I couldn't fit in both mountain climbing and scuba diving if I wanted to succeed in either. One summer I had the opportunity to teach mountain climbing in Switzerland. This led me to eventually start a mountain climbing and survival school. This couldn't have happened if I spent summertime dabbling in scuba diving and mountain climbing.

Let me continue my story. After six years I closed the climbing school because I wasn't making enough money to live comfortably. What was the problem? I had a very good education. I had college degree, even a master's degree in education. I had lots of opportunities to try things and learn things as I grew up. Something was not right. What was it? I learned the answer when I had children of my own.

As our children got older, my wife and I decided to home school them. This caused me to realize there is something far more important to children than lots of learning experiences. It is, quite simply, character development. It is not experience per se that prepares a child for adult responsibilities. There is no guarantee that any experience we give our children will actually prepare them in any way.

It may surprise you to learn that proper education is not broadening the child's experience. It is narrowing the child's experience in order to focus on character development. It is far more important for the child to learn diligence, mastering a subject, learning to work, and being self-governing rather than having broad experience in life. Diligence and work mean a child needs to really learn to master one or two things. A child who has learned the art of mastering a subject (academic and also in the broader sense) is prepared and able to master other subjects. The child has learned to think and not just act on emotions. The child has learned to sacrifice some things in order to gain more important things. In short, mastering a subject means the child has learned to be self-governing in this area. A child who has learned to govern himself can then apply himself to master new areas of life. Then when they are put in new situations as an adult, they are equipped to succeed.

Perhaps you don't agree or not convinced with what I am saying but let me tell you about my daughter who was home schooled. During the first six months of homeschooling, we didn't do much academically. Why? Because we first needed to teach her how to work. And we needed to learn how to teach! I remember telling her to clean the bathroom. But what does that really mean? My wife explained that we needed to show her what cleaning the bathroom meant. (Thank goodness for discerning wives!) We taught my daughter to clean the sinks, the counters, the mirrors, etc. Then we let her practice it and helped her improve until she did an acceptable job. Then we let her practice diligence by assigning this task to her.

Finally, we started the academic subjects. I was responsible to teach science and math. I asked her what grades she expected to earn in math. She thought she would only get C's or D's for grades. Of course, that just means a failure to master the subject. Accepting a grade of C means the student hasn't mastered the lesson enough to proceed to the next lesson. That's why children fail to succeed in math as they get older. Math builds on itself and failure to master one level guarantees failure at succeeding levels. Does that sound familiar?

The first math lesson I gave my daughter she only got a C. Surprise! She had to do the lesson over because she hadn't mastered the subject matter. It didn't take long for her to realize I was serious about mastering the lesson. We always took whatever time was necessary for her to understand the material. She quickly learned to be diligent, hard-working, and competent. She learned it was better to focus on doing the lesson well the first time rather than try to rush through all the lessons just to say you've had the experience. It's not the experience of doing lessons that was important. It was mastering the subject!

When my daughter became an adult, she was a manager of a retail store in the Galleria Mall in Houston She was responsible for hiring and training staff. Much to her surprise, most young people (only a few years younger than her) didn't know the meaning of work. They expected rewards and advancement without having earned either. All the broadening of their experiences as a child failed to teach them how to succeed in life!

Humans have been around for thousands of years and some cultures many hundreds of years. Sometimes we can learn from the wisdom they have accumulated through experience, trial and error, and observation. I don't think many people would argue with the need to train children. But it is very interesting that the Hebrew word for "train" comes from a primitive root meaning to narrow. This is just the opposite of what we would expect today. The purpose of education is not to broaden the child's horizon or to give him lots of experience to prepare him for life. It is to narrow or focus the child so he can learn to succeed in life. A child can succeed in life when he has learned to be self-governing. He has learned to think, not be swayed by emotion, and learned to sacrifice desire for a better future. These are internal attributes that cannot be bought, sold, lost, or found and is part of the character of the person regardless of the vicissitudes of life.

Our culture has led us to focus on our youth and youthfulness. Our prosperity convinces us we are going in the right direction doing the right thing. But we have not taken the time to give our children what they need to succeed. Sometimes this means not giving them what they want. The truth is, we haven't always acted as responsible adults because of our mistaken beliefs. The predictable result is that it has made it very difficult for our children to become responsible, successful adults.

We have set our will to help our children by giving them lots of opportunity for varied experiences. But we haven't taken the time to think this through carefully. We have just accepted uncritically that education means broadening a child's experiences. Unfortunately, our uncritical thinking has put us to fighting reality. That's not very virtuous!

Our society and our education system have forgotten the true purpose of education: teaching children to be mature. Maturity always involves sacrifice and narrowing ourselves to

accomplish what needs to be done. We can't succeed otherwise
– either as individuals or as a society.

Virtue and Meaning

Do you like to eat? I expect you do. I know I certainly do! And I must confess I sometimes like to eat junk food. Sour cream and onion potato chips seem to be my current indulgence. That and chocolate pastry! Does that make me a bad person? I don't think so. But talking of food leads me to an interesting observation.

--- Okay, I'm back from indulging in a few potato chips. What's my interesting observation? I need food as we all do and this has no inherent moral quality. It's neither good or bad. But that's not true of my food choices. They are decidedly good or bad. My current love of potato chips doesn't give me a lot of good nutrition. Rather, the chips give me lots of fat and starch and make me overweight. Ugh. But they sure taste good! Yes, I have a need for food, but it is my choices that have a moral character. They really are either good or bad choices.

As I think more about needs, I realize we all need food, water, air, and shelter. But after that what other universal needs do humans share? I think there is an important one missing from my list. Consider the fact that we all seek meaning in our lives. One of the dangers of depression comes from feeling that life doesn't matter. It's meaningless. Without meaning, suicide seems like a good option.

Humans have a very difficult time tolerating meaningless lives. It simply can't be sustained. Even the bum on the street has the drive to get his next drink. But if he ever starts feeling hopeless and his life is meaningless, he won't go on living for very long. It may never have occurred to you that this is what distinguishes us from other animals. In the past language was thought to make us unique. Then it was the use of tools. Simply playing was even suggested but you just have to watch otters at play to know this doesn't make us special. None of these proved to be unique to humans. It is only the need for meaning that makes us unique.

Interestingly, there doesn't seem to be any biological (evolutionary) reason for the need for meaning. But can you see how it motivates us in our social interactions? Much of the meaning we get in life comes from our interactions with other people. Sure, we can get meaning from an individual activity, but we are inherently social creatures. We desire the presence of other people. This deserves closer study.

Think about your life for a moment. What gives your life meaning? Is it family, friends, work, social clubs, or church? Maybe it's politics, environmental activism, or some other worthy cause. Whatever the many and varied activities are, they are important to you because they give meaning to your life. That's why you choose to do them. Please remember needs are not inherently moral. Your need to have meaning in life is not inherently moral. But your choices are moral and since they are your choices, you consider them good. Of course, this makes them virtuous choices in your sight.

Do you see a problem with this? We make choices to give meaning to our lives and this has a positive effect. We assume the positive effect makes our choices virtuous. But think about the people who supported Stalin? This gave meaning to life for a lot of them but only at the expense of millions of other peoples' lives. That was evil. It was not virtuous. Generally, Stalin's supporters didn't think their choices were evil. They were just the choices that gave meaning to their lives. Inevitably, this made them virtuous choices in their own sight because they were blind to the truth.

I want to remind you there can be no virtue when there is no absolute truth. There are just choices. But be honest. Our human nature lets us easily say our choices are virtuous. And it lets us say opposing choices are not just wrong, they are evil. And compromise with evil is not a virtue. How then can there be a conversation about virtue? I'm right and virtuous. You're wrong and evil. To think otherwise calls into question the very things that give my life meaning!

Now do you see why we are having a difficult time in America? We do not have a common ground about the things that bring meaning to our lives. And we won't have a discussion about virtue because this threatens the value of the very things that give us meaning. It is as though we are doomed to failure. But there is hope.

Right now, we need to learn an important secret. We can have a discussion or even a strong debate about virtue without destroying meaning in our lives. On the contrary, it lets us define virtue in a way that better matches reality. Ultimately this will make our lives more meaningful. Why? Because it makes our choices fit better to reality and that's real virtue.

We cannot afford to blindly hold onto our choices out of fear of losing meaning in our lives. We need to be more positive about life. We must be willing to strive for more meaningful lives. In past chapters I have tried to show you how our choices have not been very virtuous. But surely, we can do better if we are willing to change. Americans CAN do this.

I have suggested the Golden Rule is a good start towards defining virtue. What do you think? Don't be threatened and don't be dogmatic. Be open to the possibility of positive change. Let's start the discussion and together build a better America!

Hope

Is America's day of judgment coming? Maybe. But now is not the time for us to be fatalistic. There is hope. People can and do change. Societies can and do change. All the many problems discussed throughout this book were created by people, which means people can solve them. We can only do this as we come together collectively with a clear vision and a clear objective.

Yes, we must act collectively to solve our problems. But did you notice that the solutions to our problems must start with individual change? Pride, presumption, idolatry, entitlement, greed, envy, immaturity, magical thinking are all problems individuals have. It is individuals who must willingly forgo these. It is the individual who must be virtuous and apply the Golden Rule. But what do we see happening in our society today?

More and more our society focuses on group identity and group guilt. Just look at how black conservatives are vilified as uncle toms. Christians are called homophobes and bigots. Men are taught to fight against their toxic masculinity and confess their sins. And so on it goes throughout society. All these focus on collective guilt and collective redemption. And this distorts virtue.

No longer is virtue seen as an individual characteristic. It is considered a characteristic of the group. Naturally, this means the individual must conform to the group. And that's the heart of the problem. The individual no longer has to be virtuous. He or she just needs to conform to the group to be considered virtuous. It's no longer necessary to struggle with applying the Golden Rule in specific situations. It's no longer how do I love my neighbor as myself. Instead, it becomes the argument of the Pharisees: who is my neighbor? This is a much simpler question for us to answer. It's just not the right question.

The truth is life is not simple. The temptation is always there for me to give some group the responsibility to determine virtue. But history shows us that groups are not always virtuous. They aren't because the individuals comprising the group aren't virtuous. There's no getting around this fact. Reality is what it is. Pretending otherwise only leads us into fantasy. Groups get their virtue from the individuals in the group. It is individuals that must be virtuous and practice virtue in their lives. Individuals don't inherit virtue from a group. Instead, they give virtue to it!

Take heart. This means there is hope for America. Disaster is not inevitable. We don't have to be like children swayed by emotions. Nor do we need to be willful adults foregoing critical thinking. We can forsake magical thinking and choose to be mature people practicing virtue. The Golden Rule is a good place to start. Then we can come together collectively in a way that can solve real problems rather than compound them.

At its heart, this book is a call to individuals to help solve our collective problems by practicing individual virtue. This is how to build a better future. There is no shortcut we can take to get there otherwise. Throughout each day each one of us chooses to practice virtue or not. The sum total of all these individual decisions has a great influence on America's future, for better or worse. This prompts me to ask one last question. Are you willing to change to make a better future together? The answer you give can bring much hope!